Rethinking Federal
Housing Policy

Rethinking Federal Housing Policy

How to Make Housing
Plentiful and Affordable

Edward L. Glaeser

Joseph Gyourko

The AEI Press

Publisher for the American Enterprise Institute
WASHINGTON, D.C.

Distributed to the Trade by National Book Network, 15200 NBN Way, Blue Ridge
Summit, PA 17214. To order call toll free 1-800-462-6420 or 1-717-794-3800.
For all other inquiries please contact the AEI Press, 1150 Seventeenth Street, N.W.,
Washington, D.C. 20036 or call 1-800-862-5801.

NRI NATIONAL
RESEARCH
INITIATIVE

This publication is a project of the National Research Initiative, a program of the
American Enterprise Institute that is designed to support, publish, and disseminate
research by university-based scholars and other independent researchers who are
engaged in the exploration of important public policy issues.

Library of Congress Cataloging-in-Publication Data

Glaeser, Edward L. (Edward Ludwig), 1967-
  Rethinking federal housing policy : how to make housing plentiful and
affordable / Edward L. Glaeser and Joseph Gyourko.
    p. cm.
  Includes bibliographical references and index.
  ISBN-13: 978-0-8447-4273-1
  ISBN-10: 0-8447-4273-2
  1. Housing policy—United States. 2. Housing—Prices—United States.
I. Gyourko, Joseph E., 1956– II. Title.

  HD7293.G5 2008
  363.5'820973--dc22

                                                            2008040992
12 11 10 09 08   1 2 3 4 5

Printed in the United States of America

*This book is dedicated to
Edmund Chaitman and Joseph Gyourko, Jr.,
our fathers, in gratitude for
their inspiration and guidance.*

Contents

List of Illustrations

TABLES

Acknowledgments

We thank Henry Olsen for inspiring this work, two anonymous reviewers for very helpful comments, and Jim Poterba for his considerable insight into American housing and tax policy. As always, our home institutions, the Taubman Center for State and Local Government at Harvard University and the Zell/Lurie Real Estate Center at the Wharton School of the University of Pennsylvania, provided the supportive intellectual environment needed to complete this project. Finally, Andrew Moore and Cristiano Costa provided excellent research assistance.

Authors' Note

This manuscript was completed before Fannie Mae and Freddie Mac were taken over by the federal government. While some revisions have been made to reflect this change, our book is not intended to be a critique of those two government-sponsored enterprises or of the mortgage finance system in general. We provide a more broad-based evaluation of the many different types of policies intended to promote housing affordability, only a few of which work through the mortgage market. One of the lessons from our analysis is that Fannie Mae and Freddie Mac did little to make housing more affordable. The prime beneficiaries of these institutions were their management and shareholders until just before their collapse, not the taxpayers or even middle-income homebuyers.

The current housing crisis is indeed something of an indictment of the entire existing housing policy edifice. Policies have focused on supporting housing demand through tax breaks and cheaper credit, while allowing housing supply to get ever more restricted in many areas of the country. Subsidizing demand when supply is fixed not only leads to higher prices but also enables greater housing price volatility. Historically, the most painful price swings have been in places where new construction is restricted. If federal agencies push demand-side aid, such as easy credit, when prices are high, then this aid will only exacerbate the swing of the housing price cycle.

Paul Romer was right: "A crisis is a terrible thing to waste." The demise of Fannie Mae and Freddie Mac provides the opportunity to rethink housing affordability policy more generally. It is essential that we learn from past mistakes, which have been plentiful and costly, and which go well beyond those that will be associated with restructuring Fannie and Freddie. We argue for a clearer diagnosis of the underlying problem, which inevitably leads to a focus on local government restrictions on new building that limit supply and help push prices up in our most expensive markets. The very nature of the recent bust in housing prices cannot be fully comprehended without understanding the role of local supply constraints. Not only are the supply-constrained markets on our coasts the most expensive, but they are more volatile, experiencing greater boom and bust cycles, both now and in the past.

We propose a specific new policy designed to counter the overly restrictive building policies of many local governments—one, we hope, upon which new policies for a recovering housing and mortgage market may be built.

Edward L. Glaeser and Joseph Gyourko
October 22, 2008

Introduction

Over the past fifty years, American homes have increased dramatically in size and quality. By historical and international standards, the homes now being built are extraordinary, and prices remain moderate in those places where construction is abundant. Yet despite these successes, America also faces two troubling affordability problems. The first is that the truly disadvantaged are too poor to afford housing even if it is inexpensively provided. The second is that in a small but growing number of metropolitan areas, housing prices have soared, making housing unaffordable even for middle-income Americans.

In the short run, both problems will be eased by the emerging cyclical downturn in the housing markets. Housing prices themselves are cyclical; this is shown in figure I-1, which plots the (log) real constant-quality house price index for the nation over a more than thirty-year period using data from the Office of Federal Housing Enterprise Oversight (OFHEO). But this cyclicality itself implies that any price reductions will be temporary. Without major changes in housing policy, prices will come roaring back in a matter of years. When prices rise again in the future, some metropolitan areas will become increasingly off-limits for all but a small number of wealthy home buyers.

Can federal policy ease this problem? The national government long has played a significant role in American housing markets, ostensibly to help make housing more affordable. Local governments play an even more important role in directing new construction, but some of them clearly are not trying to ease the burden of high housing prices. In this volume, we review America's existing housing policies and ask how they can be improved to make housing markets function more efficiently and housing itself more affordable.

The affordability debate historically has been dominated by the question of how to house the poor. A half century ago, improving the housing

1

FIGURE I-1

NATIONAL CONSTANT-QUALITY REAL HOUSE PRICE INDEX, 1975–2007

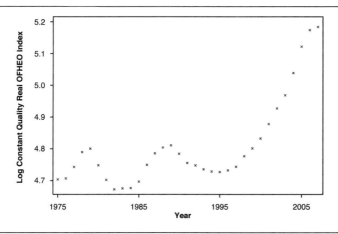

SOURCE: Office of Federal Housing Enterprise Oversight. Repeat Sales House Price Index. Washington, D.C.: U.S. Census Bureau, 1993–2008.

of the less fortunate required policymakers to acknowledge that the poor often resided in dilapidated units without basic essentials such as indoor plumbing with hot water. In those days, the low quality of the housing stock was a big part of the problem, not just the poor's inability to pay for it (Frieden 1968). Fortunately, dilapidated units as conventionally defined are now a very small part of the housing stock, and America's housing generally is of quite good quality (see chapter 2 for those data). However, poverty itself remains. If we want poorer Americans to be able to afford good housing, we will have to decide the best way to address their lack of financial resources.

The second affordability problem is newer and more complicated. While housing prices certainly have boomed over the last decade, much of the U.S. housing market is still working well, providing abundant housing at prices close to the costs of construction. In those areas, housing costs still can be a burden to the poorest Americans, but this is a function of their poverty, not of any intrinsic failure of the housing market. However, in a small but growing set of markets, including coastal California and various East Coast areas, the housing market is failing to produce affordable homes. Prices have become extraordinarily high and there is little new construction.

The combination of robust demand and limited new supply makes these areas increasingly unaffordable to middle-class households, not only the poor.

While the provision of excessive and mispriced mortgage debt is the key factor behind the recent boom and bust in housing markets, the extraordinary nature of this cycle cannot be fully understood without acknowledging the role that both demand-side policies and supply constraints played in what happened. The boom in housing prices was certainly exacerbated by policies that made credit cheaper, especially for lower-income borrowers. As prices rose, the government-sponsored enterprises (GSEs) became more aggressive in supporting lending, which contributed further to the price rise. The subsequent collapse of Fannie Mae and Freddie Mac has contributed to the current decline in housing prices.

While demand-side policies can increase the volatility of housing prices, policies that make supply more elastic can reduce that volatility. Housing prices are much more volatile in markets where supply is constrained by regulation (Glaeser, Gyourko, and Saiz 2008). In well-functioning markets, both price and quantity can adjust to changes in demand conditions. In supply-constrained markets, most of the adjustment occurs in the price of housing because stringent land-use regulations make it too costly to change the quantity of housing very much. The absence of supply adjustment makes these markets more volatile over time, both on the upside and downside of the cycle. Hence, housing supply restrictions, not just problems in the mortgage market, help account for the magnitude of the price movements that we see in the nation's coastal markets especially.

Glaeser, Gyourko, and Saiz (2008) argue that price bubbles are more likely to form in highly regulated markets because a very tight, or inelastic, supply of homes is needed to support the increasingly large price increases that sustain a bubble whenever demand is rising. It is more difficult for home prices to become disconnected from their fundamental production costs in markets where plentiful supply is forthcoming whenever prices rise much above those costs. In fact, housing construction jumped during the housing boom of the early to middle 1980s in these more elastically supplied markets such as Atlanta, and prices remained quite close to production costs throughout the cycle. It was the level of construction activity, not prices, that varied most over the cycle in the freer, more unregulated markets. The more recent boom did see a few such markets (e.g., Orlando,

Phoenix, Las Vegas) experience temporary price jumps, but the length of their booms still is much shorter than in the more tightly regulated, supply-constrained coastal markets. Between 1996 and 2006, average real house price growth was forty-seven percentage points greater in the more supply-constrained markets: 81 percent real appreciation in the constrained markets versus 34 percent in the less-constrained ones.

The recent boom was widespread, but it was also much larger in the more regulated coastal markets, which indicates that housing supply conditions, not just demand factors associated with incomes and mortgage markets, play an important role in accounting for the very nature of booms and busts in different areas of the country. This also suggests that sound policy to counter overly restrictive local regulation of new construction can have benefits beyond those directly associated with making housing more affordable.

Federal policy certainly has the potential to make these areas more affordable because their lack of affordability is itself the result of government action. The limited supply of new homes in these high-cost areas does not reflect intrinsic barriers to supply. In fact, many of these areas built vast amounts of housing less than a generation ago. Instead, an increasingly dense web of local government land-use regulations has made it very difficult to build in these high-cost places.

The current collapse of the housing market and of traditional mainstays of federal housing policy like Freddie Mac and Fannie Mae calls for a radical rethinking of housing policy. This is exactly the right time to reevaulate how the federal government can make housing more affordable without new institutions which will put future taxpayers in jeopardy. The first step is to recognize that true affordability is more likely to come from improving supply than subsidizing demand. Today, local governments are making land-use decisions that may be in the interests of their own communities, but that are not in the interest of the nation as a whole. NIMBYism (not-in-my-backyard philosophy) may be locally popular, but it is a poor basis for national housing policy. The proper role of the federal government is to lean against the local tendency to block new projects.

The second step is for policymakers to recognize that the two distinct affordability problems warrant very different solutions. The policies that help the poor should not target spending on one market or another. The starkest example of the folly of such place-based aid can be seen in the unfortunate consequences of federal policies that created high-rise concentrations of poverty in our inner cities. The poor should have the greatest possible freedom to move wherever there is more opportunity. The best approach to achieving that aim is to directly provide them more resources, in the form of either cash or housing vouchers. What the poor truly need are those resources, not buildings in places determined by politicians or politically connected developers.

A third step toward a new housing policy that effectively addresses affordability issues is to acknowledge the vast heterogeneity of American housing markets and to understand that the same policy that works well in one market may not in another. America has three types of housing markets. In the poorer central cities of the Northeast and Midwest, housing prices are low and there is little new construction. Demand is quite low in these places. In the booming areas of Sunbelt sprawl, prices are moderate and new construction is abundant. Demand is high in these markets, but prices are kept in check by abundant private-sector supply. In the Northeast from Washington, D.C., to Boston, as well as in coastal California, prices are high and new construction is rare. These areas have robust housing demand, but very limited supply.

There is no affordability problem for middle-income Americans in either Houston or central city Detroit. Thus, any policy that sought to induce new construction in these areas would be either wasteful or ineffective. This same policy applied to San Francisco, however, would help the middle class by increasing the supply of housing units. It is easy to understand the appeal of a single national policy, but if we continue with uniform interventions that do not reflect local differences, then our future efforts are likely to be as unproductive as many of those in the past. Simply put, "one size does not fit all" must guide policy design.

In this volume, we propose an affordability policy built on the recognition that America has many different housing markets and that both demand-side and supply-side policies need to take account of that heterogeneity. Specifically, we propose that the federal government provide financial incentives for localities to permit more building in counties where prices are high and construction is low. The goal of this policy is to offset the natural tendency of these communities to restrict new construction.

We propose funding this plan with a second reform that is also grounded in the fact that American housing markets are quite distinct. This reform would fine-tune the home mortgage interest deduction, which currently has the counterproductive effect of allowing buyers to bid up house prices in areas where supply is severely restricted or inelastic. In these areas, the home mortgage interest deduction functions mainly to make housing less, not more, affordable. A particularly unfortunate distributional consequence of the deduction is that it subsidizes the demand of the wealthy, who itemize on their tax returns, and not the demand of the poor, who do not itemize. Our reform would permit individuals in those areas to deduct interest on only the first $300,000 of mortgage debt. It may make sense to phase this in over time, so that it hits only recent home buyers, not existing owners who borrowed under the old regime.

In either case, the changes in the home mortgage interest deduction will generate new revenues that can then be used to fund a program that rewards localities for building new homes. In addition, localities will have the opportunity to recoup this tax revenue if they permit building again. If enough new construction occurs, they exit the program altogether. This program reduces one demand-side force that props up housing prices in areas with inelastic supply, and uses the revenues generated to provide incentives for communities to permit more housing units.

We sketch this policy proposal more thoroughly at the end of this chapter and in the conclusion, but our main objective is not to push one specific policy. Rather, it is to emphasize that different policies are needed in different areas of the country.

The Plan of the Book

The first chapter begins by discussing the standard ability-to-pay measure of housing affordability, which is defined in terms of the ratio of income to house price. The Millennial Housing Commission, which considers housing unaffordable once a household pays more than 30 percent of income for it, reported that housing was unaffordable for 28 million households (about 25 percent of the total) in 1999 (Millennial Housing Commission 2002, 2).[1] This large number leads the commission to recommend a host of subsidy programs to improve the situation. While one can quibble with the 30 percent figure, some measure of ability to pay does make sense in defining the affordability problem faced by the poor.

However, even in the case of the poor, real income is a better indicator of social distress than any metric of housing affordability. The nation's poor households suffer from a fundamental income deficit, not from some failure in the housing market that is making apartments too expensive. Any ability-to-pay measure based on incomes and house prices is likely to confuse issues of poverty with problems in the housing market. Hence, it makes sense to keep these factors separate in discussions of housing affordability.

It is a mistake to conflate high housing prices and incomes for both the poor and the middle class. The poor cannot afford modestly priced housing even in well-functioning markets. In contrast, the earning power of middle-income Americans is solid, but housing remains unaffordable to them in the high-priced markets on the seaboards. In fact, while other durable goods such as cars and appliances have become more affordable, housing in many coastal markets has not.

We show in chapter 1 that the usual ability-to-pay metric inevitably misclassifies when and where housing is too expensive or unaffordable from the perspective of the middle class. Hence, we define housing as being "too expensive" when its price is high relative to its fundamental production costs. The reason construction costs are a good benchmark for what the price of housing should be in a well-functioning market is that, if we believe housing is too expensive in some place, then the correct response presumably is to produce more housing so that its price will fall to the level at which it can be produced in a competitive market. From our perspective as economists, the true social cost of new housing cannot be lower than its cost of construction, so for there to be a social gain from new production, housing must be priced above construction costs.

Thus, high housing prices should be evaluated not relative to incomes, but relative to the fundamentals of the housing market, construction costs in particular. We argue that direct housing-market interventions should be contemplated only when the housing market is failing to deliver homes at a price that is close to or below construction costs. The existence of people so poor that they cannot afford even inexpensive housing does not justify intervening in the housing market, whether to stimulate new supply or to regulate in different ways. The proper way to deal with poverty is to transfer resources to the impoverished, not to meddle with the housing market.

Chapter 2 documents the state of American housing. Housing consumption has increased markedly over the past quarter century, and not only for the rich. Poor people, not just the rich, are living in larger and better homes than their counterparts were thirty years ago. For example, dilapidated units defined in terms of overcrowding (especially more than 1.5 persons per room) or substandard physical characteristics (no running or hot water; holes in the structure that do not fully protect residents from the elements or that pose safety problems) largely have disappeared from the housing stock over the last three decades.

While once it was quite plausible to think that increasing the quality of housing was in the public interest, it is hard to hold that view today. Americans live in homes that are extremely large by world and historical standards. If the market for housing is failing, then that failure must lie in housing prices, not in housing quality.

Chapter 2 also documents the steady increase in housing prices in the United States generally, and the particularly dramatic price increases within a number of important and populous markets. In those areas, prices are increasingly diverging from the physical costs of construction. For example, the median quality home from the 2000 census was valued at nearly $600,000 in 2006 in the New York City metropolitan area and exceeded $650,000 in the San Francisco metropolitan area.[2] This suggests that some type of barrier to building is making housing cost substantially more than its fundamental production costs in certain markets.

Chapter 3 begins our analysis of the regulations and policies that help drive prices. We first place our current housing policies in historical context. Public safety concerns involving fire hazards and public health concerns regarding the spread of disease were the initial justifications for governmental regulation of the housing market. Modern regulation has moved away from these historical motivations toward more clearly targeted efforts to restrict supply and manage density.

One lesson from our overview of housing policy history in chapter 3 is that the half-life of any given policy tends to be very long. Many ancient policies persist despite the fact that the original rationales for them are no longer relevant. This should serve as a warning to policymakers. They would be wise to subject housing policies to sunset provisions, so that policies can be changed or terminated if the conditions that spawned them change.

Chapter 4 documents and analyzes the extant major government policies that directly try to control prices or quantities in housing markets. We look at rent control, which fortunately has been abandoned by most cities and now exists in only four states. Price controls such as this may have fallen out of favor, but the same cannot be said for quantity and quality controls, including building codes, which have become increasingly cumbersome.

Land use controls and regulation, not building codes, bear primary responsibility for restricting housing supply and boosting prices well above construction costs. Chapter 4 shows that communities throughout the country use an incredibly broad set of quantity controls to restrict the type and amount of new housing that can be built. In many cases, the courts are an important partner in this process. The front line of the battle over quantity regulation is now in suburban communities that have greatly reduced the amount of new construction through minimum-lot-size requirements and other rules. One stark example involves the sixty-acre minimum lots that exist in some pricey suburbs in Marin County.[3]

We show that house prices are materially higher in markets with stricter local land-use regulatory regimes. Data from a recent nationwide survey of land-use regulatory conditions show that prices in the areas with the strictest controls average over $130,000 more than those in areas with the average land-use control regime (Gyourko, Saiz, and Summers 2008a). This is roughly equal to the physical construction costs for a home of good quality in most markets, so the impact on prices looks to be large. The data also suggest that once the gap between house price and construction costs becomes large, there is no going back to a cheap land environment (Glaeser and Gyourko 2003).

There clearly is a legitimate role for local land-use regulation, but it is easy to understand why localities often go too far in restricting the production of new homes. Most of the benefits of new construction projects go to people who currently live outside the permitting jurisdiction (plus the current land owner, who may or may not be a local resident), while most of the so-called negative externalities (e.g., congestion, pollution) are paid by existing residents. Moreover, when a locality builds, it makes housing more affordable for everyone. For existing owners, higher prices are not a problem. Rather, new building could decrease the value of their most important asset.

Expensive housing is a problem for renters and those who want to move into high-price areas. A high cost of living also raises labor costs for firms. In larger cities such as New York and Chicago, where the competing interests of renters, business owners, and homeowners must be taken into account, mayors such as Michael Bloomberg and Richard M. Daley generally fight hard for new construction in order to ensure that workers can afford to live near the businesses that employ them. In leafy suburbs with few businesses and few renters, there is no group to oppose existing home-owners' natural desire to restrict construction. The result is inefficiently low production of housing units in those places. This is the primary market failure in housing markets today, and a new housing policy is needed to provide incentives for overly restrictive local communities to change their behavior and allow more production in desired markets.

Chapter 5 analyzes the major federal government interventions in the housing markets, which involve subsidies to the consumption and production of housing. These include the Section 8 voucher program, the federal tax expenditure program that allows homeowners to deduct mortgage interest and local property taxes, the implicit subsidies to housing-related government-sponsored enterprises, and the subsidies to housing construction for poorer families through the Low Income Housing Tax Credit (LIHTC) program. With the notable exception of the voucher program, these programs do remarkably little to make housing more affordable. Our analysis of these programs leads us to conclude that the Section 8 voucher program is the only truly bright spot in federal housing policy over the past three decades. All but the voucher program could be eliminated without materially worsening affordability conditions on average. In some situations, eliminating the programs actually would improve affordability for many households.

It may seem surprising that local, not national, policy on housing supply really influences whether the nonpoor can afford housing. Mortgage interest deductibility and the two housing-related GSEs—the Federal National Mortgage Association (FNMA or Fannie Mae) and the Federal Home Loan Mortgage Corporation (FHLMC or Freddie Mac)—certainly are more visible. These demand-side interventions targeted at the middle class are huge and help households buy more housing than they would otherwise. However, they are not what makes housing affordable, and their absence would not engender an affordability crisis. Some people would want to own a different (smaller) home if mortgage interest was not deductible, but it is unlikely that ownership rates would significantly change even if no mortgage interest was deductible.

Chapter 5 also emphasizes that any given program will affect different markets in different ways depending on local supply conditions. For example, we show that the home mortgage interest deduction does not lower the costs of owning in markets where new housing construction is constrained, even if prices rise above construction costs. Economic forces ensure that the value of the tax benefit is capitalized into higher land values, making housing more, not less, expensive in those areas. Thus, the main beneficiaries of the favorable tax treatment of owner-occupied housing in the high-cost markets on both coasts are the existing owners, not new or future home buyers.

The LIHTC program has the potential to improve affordability conditions for the poor by increasing supply through its subsidy to developers of low-income housing. However, current research finds that the LIHTC is not very effective along any important dimension—other than to benefit developers and their investors. Because the program has uniform national participation requirements, it wastes substantial resources by subsidizing construction in markets with plentiful new supply and no underlying affordability crisis. Essentially, the subsidized construction crowds out many units that would have been provided by the private sector in the absence of the program. Economic analysis, we show in chapter 5, makes clear that the program has little impact on the rents paid by the poor. The program functions so that the prime beneficiaries are the recipients of the tax credits, not poor renters. Consequently, we recommend eliminating the LIHTC program, although we clearly see the need for a different and better-designed supply program.

If Fannie Mae and Freddie Mac had as little impact on middle-class housing affordability as our analysis suggests, then their implicit government subsidy clearly was not worth the risk to the taxpayers. That said, we do not make any strong recommendations regarding changes to Fannie Mae or Freddie Mac, especially in the near term. In the midst of a severe credit crisis, we certainly do not feel qualified to advise the Treasury on whether these entities are needed to maintain essential liquidity in the mortgage market. When more normal conditions return, it seems sensible to separate the affordable housing mission from the need to provide cost-effective mortgage liquidity to middle-class households. The former should be a government responsibility and should be brought on its balance sheet. The latter should be done by the private sector, although we recognize that market conditions are far from normal as we write. The two missions are very different, should not be confused, and should not be combined in quasi-private companies in a way that allows affordable housing goals to be funded off–balance sheet from the government's perspective. We have now learned that is a recipe for disaster.

In sum, chapters 4 and 5 tell us that the overall success of the housing market has little to do with the main federal interventions, but the failure of certain markets to provide affordable housing is largely due to local government interventions that restrict new supply. The abundant inexpensive housing in the Sunbelt markets is the result of a well-functioning private-sector construction industry, not government subsidies. The lack of affordable housing in coastal California and the Northeast is the result of robust demand colliding with limited supply, with the supply constraints due more to manmade regulation than to some natural or geographic limitation.

Thus, we are at an interesting moment in the history of American housing policy, where the greatest failures of housing markets are themselves the result of government intervention, most prominently local government restrictions on new supply. The best way to make housing more affordable for millions of Americans is to fight the local land-use restrictions that limit housing supply. This can and should be supplemented with revisions to existing policy that do not result in a waste of resources or, even worse, that inadvertently make housing less affordable.

Our Proposal

We conclude the book by proposing housing policy reforms that incorporate all these lessons. The best means of helping the poor who find housing unaffordable is to give them more resources. A sensible policy would be substantially simpler than the current cluster of federal housing policies. Its goal would be to provide the poor as efficiently as possible with sufficient resources to achieve whatever level of housing consumption society deems appropriate.

The simplest version of such a policy would be a negative income tax that had no particular connection to housing markets (Friedman 1962). If society wishes the subsidy to be in-kind, then housing vouchers are recommended, as they have been found to be much cheaper than production subsidies to build housing units (U.S. GAO 2002). Supply-side policies that encourage new construction for the poor not only are flawed conceptually, but have severe implementation problems. After all, the government itself rarely is a good developer. Lower-cost housing is much more likely to be old housing than new housing, and if we are trying to provide more low-cost housing for the poor, it makes little sense to focus on building more new homes.

In contrast, a focus on supply is critical for the middle-class affordability problem, because insufficient supply of housing units lies at the heart of this growing issue. Increasing the supply of housing is the only way to make coastal America more affordable, but the government has a poor track record of stimulating supply. Public construction generally has been a failure. The Low Income Housing Tax Credit program is only marginally more successful, and we recommend scrapping that program altogether. Thus, history seems to warn against both direct public provision of homes and targeted tax subsidies for developers.

Basic economics as well as history warns against implementing uniform housing policies across the United States. America is a big country with tremendous variation in housing markets. Many of these markets have no affordability problem for middle-income people. There is no reason to have a federal policy that encourages housing supply in these areas. Supply-side housing policy should be limited to areas with high housing values and limited production of new homes. In our analysis, these areas have average prices near $400,000 in today's dollars and new construction that adds less than 1 percent a year to their existing stock of housing. Markets like this exist in eight states, and are concentrated in California, Massachusetts, New Jersey, and New York.

Since local land-use policies are the primary reason that high-cost areas do not have enough new development, federal government policy should focus on counteracting these local limitations on construction. Under our plan, the federal government will provide funding tied to new construction. For each new home that a community permits, it will receive a significant amount of increased aid. The actual programs will be designed by states, subject to three conditions. All payments can go only to local government, which can use them either for basic spending needs or to reduce taxes. All payments must be tied to new construction. And continued funding of the program depends on increasing housing production at the county level.

The program will be financed by changing the home mortgage interest deduction in areas where housing is in inelastic supply. Reducing the size of the deduction in those areas with high costs and limited supply not only will make housing more affordable, it will provide a means of funding the local aid-for-new-homes program in a way that involves no redistribution across space. Localities will be paying for their own increases in government aid with the increased tax revenues that result from reducing the home mortgage interest deduction.

The reduction we propose in high-cost, low-supply areas caps deductions at $300,000 of mortgage debt. This would affect fewer than one in twenty owners. Those who would be affected live disproportionately in the housing markets with the highest prices and the tightest constraints on new construction. The cap would be waived for borrowers in all other markets. The additional taxes that the federal government would collect from large mortgage borrowers in these inelastically supplied markets then would be rebated to the local governments to encourage new housing construction under the three conditions described above. It is also possible that the cap could be higher for existing mortgages and apply mainly to new home buyers.

Calculations reported in appendix 2 indicate that the revenues generated by this program would be large enough to substantially increase the supply of homes in the high-priced markets where presently there is very little new supply. Even assuming $30,000 as the amount required to convince a locality to allow one more housing unit construction permit, the funding is significant enough to more than double permitting rates in many markets. Essentially, this program allows the local community to keep more of the benefits that accrue from allowing more growth and to decide how best to alleviate any of the harm associated with it. Because local governments have created the massive undersupply in America's most expensive markets, we must change the behavior of those local governments by changing the incentives they face to approve new residential development.

We believe that this approach makes much more sense than current alternative proposals such as the National Affordable Housing Trust Fund, which is intended to provide a new source of federal funding for building more low-income housing. This proposal repeats old mistakes and incorporates virtually none of the lessons we should have learned from past policy. It still distributes resources across all types of markets, including those where it makes no sense to subsidize construction. Problems of poverty remain confused with failures in the housing market. And the fiscal risk to the nation of combining housing affordability and mortgage liquidity goals in only quasi-private firms receiving implicit government subsidies should be clear to all after the failures of Fannie Mae and Freddie Mac. We are far better off focusing on housing vouchers and freeing private developers from local interference than attempting again to micromanage subsidized supply or to reconstitute a large role for the two major housing agencies.

1

How Do We Know When Housing Is "Affordable"?

A consensus seems to have arisen that housing becomes "unaffordable" when costs rise above 30 percent of household income. This is not only the standard used by the Millennial Housing Commission in its recent report, but also is the basis for a number of U.S. Department of Housing and Urban Development (HUD) policies. Thirty percent is the threshold share of income that voucher recipients are required to contribute toward renting their units. The maximum rent that developers can charge on units financed under the LIHTC program is 30 percent of the income maximum for subsidized renters. We will discuss the details of these programs later. In this chapter, we take issue with both the 30 percent figure and with the idea that housing affordability is best judged by comparing housing costs with income.

Combining income and housing costs in a single affordability metric is a bad idea because it confuses issues of income inequality with problems in the housing market. To better understand why, consider a head of a household earning the $7.25 minimum wage that will apply in the summer of 2009. Working forty hours a week for fifty weeks a year generates a pretax income of $14,500. Homeownership virtually is out of the question because little can be saved for a down payment out of such a low income. Even if that earner pays $600 per month in rent, there will be very little left for consumption of anything other than housing. By any reasonable measure, $600 dollars per month in rent is not unduly expensive; yet it will not be affordable to someone earning the minimum wage. There is no way that producing more housing will change this situation because this is a poverty problem, not a housing problem. If society wants poor households with this level of income (or less) to consume more housing, it has to transfer resources to them. Low incomes call for a poverty-related response, such as the Earned Income Tax Credit, and perhaps also for in-kind transfers such as health care and housing vouchers.

Housing policy is much better suited to deal with failures specific to the housing market than it is to fight more general social problems. A better approach to affordability is to ask whether housing prices are close to construction costs and whether those construction costs are themselves made artificially high by problems in the housing market. An income standard of affordability makes particularly little sense in cross-city comparisons. As we discuss just below, the most basic model of urban economics predicts significant differences across space in the ratio of income to housing costs, even when the housing market is functioning perfectly.

Poverty and Housing Affordability

It is easy to understand how something like a 30 percent of income standard was established. A poor household earning $15,000 per year cannot afford some of the basic necessities of life such as food, clothing, and transportation if it is spending half its income ($7,500) on shelter. If that family was paying only 30 percent of its income ($4,500) on housing, then its after-housing income would increase by $3,000, and life would get a little bit easier. Basic humanity seems to call out for intervention in the housing market to ease the burden of poor households.

The economist considering this example maintains that the same results can be achieved simply by giving the family an extra $3,000 and leaving the housing market alone. Why get involved with the housing market at all, if the real goal is to give poor people more resources? There is a case for in-kind transfers, which we will discuss later, but those transfers generally are less efficient at reducing income inequality than pure cash transfers.

Fighting inequality via policies to make housing more affordable necessarily interferes with the choices that poor people make. When the government gives the poor housing vouchers, it becomes impossible for them to spend less on housing and more on something else. In addition, if housing affordability policies involve supply-side subsidies that create "affordable" units via tax breaks for developers or inclusionary zoning rules, then the policies target the truly disadvantaged even less effectively. When developers have some input into allocating their below-market-rate units, they may well target them to the richest among those eligible for the apartments. While we can be pretty sure that the benefits associated with a pure income-redistribution program such as the Earned Income Tax Credit are reaped primarily by their poorer recipients, we can also be pretty sure that the Low Income Housing Tax Credit program yields large benefits to the developers who fight for them.[1]

Using an income threshold for housing costs to address income inequality can have unfortunate unintended consequences, including adverse incentive effects. To see this more clearly, we return to our example of a family earning $15,000 per year in a community where free market rents are $7,500 per year. A 30 percent rule implies that this family receives $3,000 in housing aid per year, leaving $10,500 per year in after-housing funds. A family earning $20,000 per year facing the same rule would receive $1,500 per year in housing aid and have $14,000 per year in after-housing income. Note that a $5,000 increase in income is associated with only a $3,500 increase in after-housing earnings. There are many reasons to think that society benefits when poor people face strong incentives to earn more income, yet those incentives are surely weakened by an implicit 30 percent tax on extra earnings.

Larger problems with this housing affordability metric arise when we move away from the very poor and calculate affordability not using rock-bottom housing costs, but those that average people actually face. For example, if we see two middle-income families in the same area, one spending 25 percent of its income on housing, and the other spending 35 percent, does this indicate a housing affordability problem for the second family? Can we say that the affordability problem has increased in severity if more people choose to spend 35 percent of their incomes on housing?

While we certainly can conclude that these households would be better off if housing cost them less, there is no reason to think that 30 percent is some sort of magic threshold. There is also no a priori reason to be troubled if some families decide to spend 35 or 40 percent of their earnings on housing. If these families choose to spend more on their homes, the job of a housing policy should be neither to restrict their choices nor to make their housing artificially inexpensive. The 30 percent threshold sheds little light on the actual functioning of the housing market, and confuses poverty, housing costs, and housing consumption decisions. A better approach is to focus on each outcome separately.

Affordability across Space

The 30 percent threshold is particularly problematic for comparisons across markets, especially when discussing the burgeoning middle-class affordability issue. That Americans are highly mobile is one of the reasons. More than 16 percent changed residences between 2005 and 2006, and more than 6 percent moved across counties in the same year (U.S. Census Bureau 2006a). The economic approach to cities and regions infers from this mobility that high housing prices are balanced by high income levels or a pleasant quality of life. Moreover, this balance does not imply that people in different places should or will be paying a constant fraction of their income on housing. In fact, giving housing aid to people in high-cost areas to the point where they are spending only 30 percent of their income on housing is likely to be both inequitable and inefficient.

This essential insight can be demonstrated with the following simple example comparing two metropolitan areas with homes of the same quality but with different levels of productivity.[2] In the first market, the average household earns $50,000 per year and homes costs $100,000 each. Further assume that interest, maintenance, and taxes amount to 10 percent of the value of the home. This is the annual user cost of occupying the home for a year, and it amounts to $10,000 (0.1 × $100,000) in this case. Abstracting from any complications associated with changing housing prices or incomes, the household has $40,000 left over to spend on other goods ($50,000 – $10,000 = $40,000).

In the second metropolitan area, productivity is higher so that average households earn $75,000. We assume that all other aspects of these two communities—such as school quality or the weather—are identical. Since people are mobile, they would naturally come to the high-income area unless high housing costs held them back. The standard economic approach to cities implies that incomes net of housing costs need to be equal across space. If they are not, then people will crowd into the high-income area.

This means that the $25,000 difference in household incomes must be off-set by a $250,000 difference in housing costs, given the 10 percent user cost of housing we assume. That is, if after-housing incomes are to be equalized across space, then the average house must cost $350,000 in the high-income area. With house prices of $350,000 and annual costs equal to 10 percent of house value (or $35,000), after-housing income is $40,000 ($75,000 − $35,000 = $40,000), which is identical to that in the first market.

In the less productive, low-cost region, households are spending 20 per-cent of their incomes on housing each year ($10,000/$50,000 = 0.2). In the high-cost region, households are spending almost 50 percent of their incomes on housing annually ($35,000/$75,000 = 0.47). An affordability measure based on the ratio of income to house price suggests that the low-cost region is highly affordable, while the high-cost region is unaffordable. But this is clearly not so. People earn the same after-housing incomes in the two areas, as indeed they would have to in order for them to be willing to live in either area. Households are equally well-off in either market. They live in the same quality house and have the same after-housing income to spend on other goods. Thus, there is no meaningful sense in which housing is less affordable, nor is there an affordability crisis, in the second market. Nobody in that market has any incentive to leave for the cheaper market (presuming they earn the average income in each market, of course).

Our example is not extreme. Average income differences of $25,000 across metropolitan areas are common, and they are generally offset by big differences in housing costs. For example, family income averaged just over $107,000 in the San Francisco primary metropolitan area in 2000, accord-ing to the decennial census for that year, compared to about $75,000 in Dallas and Atlanta and only about $66,000 in Phoenix. The gap in housing prices between San Francisco and Atlanta is larger than that implied by dif-ferences in their local incomes (assuming a user cost of capital equal to 10 percent), but there is no doubt that a significant fraction of the higher hous-ing prices in the Bay Area is due to the higher incomes earned there.[3]

Policy interventions that try to artificially reduce housing costs in the areas with high income and high housing costs are fundamentally mis-guided. Imagine a policy that gave housing support to the people in the high-cost area so that their housing costs were only 33 percent of their earnings. In this case, the after-housing income in the high-cost area would be $50,000, while the after-housing income in the low-cost area would remain at $40,000. Before the housing policy, the people in the two regions had the same disposable earnings after paying for housing costs. After the housing policy, the people in the high-income region have become appreciably better off, and inequality has increased.

The disadvantages of such a misguided affordability policy are not limited to increasing inequality across regions. The subsidy would induce people and firms to move to the high-cost region. Assuredly, this would further raise housing prices in the high-cost region, so it would be more of a bonanza to existing homeowners than a relief to renters or home buyers. None of this makes sense from a policy perspective.

In sum, very different price-to-income ratios across housing markets are normal outcomes to be expected when people are free to move across labor and housing markets. One cannot assume that those places where housing prices are a larger multiple of income are less affordable in any economically meaningful sense. Given that basic insight of urban economics, we now turn to what we believe is a more sensible way to define housing affordability.

How Should Housing Affordability Be Measured?

Whether government should try to reduce high prices has been debated in many markets, especially for oil in recent years. Of course, just because a good is expensive does not mean the government should intervene to make it cheaper. Economists generally hold that a policy response to high prices is justified only if a market failure, such as that arising from monopoly power, is making prices artificially high. No matter the cause, some reasonable benchmark is necessary if we are going to talk sensibly about affordability, and that benchmark clearly should not be an arbitrary share of an individual's income. Fortunately, in the case of housing, there is a natural measure for considering housing affordability: construction costs.

In a well-functioning housing market with competition among homebuilders, supply should be relatively elastic, and price should be determined largely by the cost of construction plus a normal profit for the builder and land assembler.[4] House values above this benchmark level signal that housing is too expensive. Developers have a strong profit incentive to supply new units to the market when prices are well above this level, so if they fail to do so, we can infer that something is standing in their way.

It also is easy to see when there is a gap between house values and construction costs, because we have data on both. Sales prices are publicly recorded, and various consultants to the construction sector provide data on what it costs to build a home in different parts of the country. These cost data surely are imperfect, and they do not include either the cost of land or some of the other soft costs involved in new construction. Yet they serve as a useful benchmark for almost all discussions of housing affordability.

Construction costs literally are the lowest price at which housing can be delivered in a given market. Hence, if prices are close to construction costs, this market is doing a good job of delivering new housing. There can be no market failure that is limiting supply and causing prices to be unduly high.

However, if house prices are significantly greater than construction costs, then we should ask why this gap exists. If the gap simply reflects the high cost of available land because of some natural scarcity, then it will be hard to narrow it without large-scale subsidization or other policies that reduce the value of land. For example, nothing the government could or should do will make land (or housing) costs the same in rural Idaho and midtown Manhattan. Conversely, if this gap reflects a market failure, such as one caused by local government policies that make new construction difficult and render developable land artificially scarce, then effective policies that bring housing costs down are easier to imagine. So, while Manhattan will never be as cheap as Idaho, it is possible to imagine that the price of Manhattan apartments could be much closer to the cost of building them.

Focusing on prices relative to construction costs, moreover, naturally also leads to far more sensible policy outcomes than we can expect from an income-based affordability measure. The long-run market price in an area inevitably reflects the interplay of supply and demand. If we want housing to cost less in an area, the most natural way to achieve that end is to increase supply. Simply put, more houses are the most straightforward way to ensure that housing is not unduly expensive.

Focusing on the gap between prices and construction costs also leads to sensible conclusions about when more housing is needed. If prices are already at or below construction costs, then there will be little room to further reduce costs with new supply unless builders are massively subsidized, and it is hard to see the rationale for that. If prices are above construction costs, then the social cost of new housing well may be lower than its value to consumers, and there can be real gains from new production.

2

The State of American Housing

In the wake of the current housing downturn, it is easy to focus on short-run events that seem to suggest great disarray in the market, but housing policy must be made for the long run. We therefore start with an overview of the housing market over the last fifty years. The long-run trends are that housing quality has increased dramatically, but so have prices. The recent decline should not blind us to the fact that prices in most markets are still substantially higher than they were at the start of the millennium. The recent wave of foreclosures should not make us think that Americans are now ill housed.

If that were the case—if too many Americans were consuming too little housing—it would provide one possible rationale for housing policy interventions. Indeed, concerns about housing consumption motivated many of the earliest interventions into the market, and vouchers are meant, at least in part, to make sure that poorer Americans have access to decent homes. Our overview of the housing market, therefore, first looks at the amount of housing that Americans are now consuming. We show that Americans are consuming very large quantities of housing, both by historical and international standards. Even poorer Americans are living in relatively large housing units compared to a generation ago.

The more troubling question is whether that housing is costing them an exorbitant amount. We look next at the price of housing across the United States. Housing prices have risen moderately in almost all metropolitan areas over the last fifteen years, but extremely high prices are a feature of only a few places. Those areas are also characterized by compensatory high incomes or attractive amenities. Still, these high prices raise concerns about housing affordability, and they will be our primary focus when we turn to policy responses that appropriately address high housing prices.

24

FIGURE 2-1

SIZE OF EXISTING RENTER- AND OWNER-OCCUPIED HOMES
(METRO AREAS, AHS NATIONAL FILES)

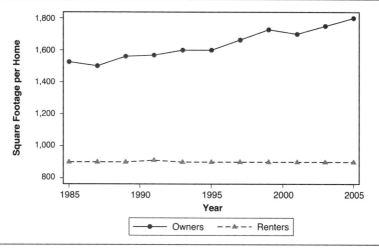

SOURCE: U.S. Census Bureau. Housing and Household Economic Statistics Division. American Housing Survey. Washington, D.C.: U.S. Census Bureau, 1985–2005.

In the previous chapter, we argued that housing prices should be deemed affordable not as a certain share of income, but relative to construction costs. In the final section of this chapter, we present data on construction costs over time and space. Over the past twenty years, these costs have not risen appreciably in real or inflation-adjusted terms, so they certainly cannot explain high and rising real house prices. Across the country, there is substantial variation in construction costs, but it cannot explain the great heterogeneity in housing prices. Finally, in high-cost areas, there is a very significant gap between home values and construction costs. This gap suggests that housing could become more affordable in high-cost areas if barriers to new construction were removed.

Housing Consumption over Time

There is no one right way to measure housing consumption. The size of the unit clearly is important, and it is the characteristic for which we have the

FIGURE 2-2

HOUSE SIZE PER PERSON

(METRO AREAS, AHS NATIONAL FILES)

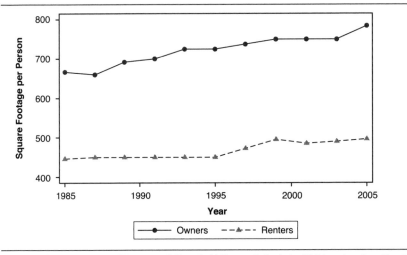

SOURCE: U.S. Census Bureau. Housing and Household Economic Statistics Division. American Housing Survey. Washington, D.C.: U.S. Census Bureau, 1985–2005.

most data. The growth in the size of newly constructed owner-occupied homes is striking. U.S. Census Bureau data show that between 1975 and 2006 the average size of a new owner-occupied home rose by 45 percent, from 1,555 ft² to 2,258 ft².[1] Americans are building much larger houses than they once did.

While new housing units give us a sense of how the housing market is changing, they do not provide us an accurate picture of the average housing unit. Most people do not live in new housing. Figure 2-1 plots data from the American Housing Survey (AHS) to show that the median size of existing rented and owner-occupied homes also has increased in the two decades since 1985, albeit by modest amounts. The growth in the size of owner-occupied homes is larger than the growth in the size of rental units.

Housing consumption per person has increased more than the growth in the median unit size because of a fall in household size. Figure 2-2 graphs median square footage per person between 1985 and 2005, again using data from the American Housing Survey. Housing consumption per

FIGURE 2-3

HOUSE SIZE PER PERSON BY INCOME QUARTILE
(UNDER AGE 55 IN METROPOLITAN STATISTICAL AREAS)

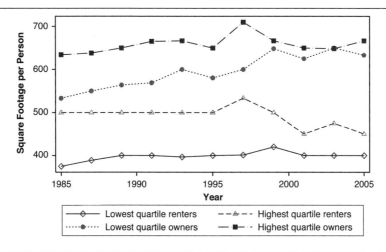

SOURCE: U.S. Census Bureau. Housing and Household Economic Statistics Division. American Housing Survey. Washington, D.C.: U.S. Census Bureau, 1985–2005.

capita among owner-occupier households now is over 700 ft^2; that for renters is about 450 ft^2.

These figures tell us only about the typical household, which can disguise important disparities across people. No one worries about whether rich Americans are consuming enough housing. However, we would be concerned if housing consumption for middle- and lower-income Americans was low or declining. To see the connection between income and housing consumption, we separately calculated average unit size per person for owners and renters, based on their income levels.

Figure 2-3 reports the average square footage of housing consumed per person for the top and bottom quartiles of the income distribution for owners and renters of working age since the AHS began reporting unit size data in 1985.[2] These data show no widening, and even a modest narrowing, of the gap in the housing space consumption of rich and poor for both owners and renters since the mid-1980s. While we do not argue that the gap truly is falling, as the modest changes depicted in figure 2-3 could be due

TABLE 2-1

COMPARISON OF U.S. HOUSING CONSUMPTION
WITH MAJOR EUROPEAN COUNTRIES

	Mean living area (ft²)		Persons per room	Per capita consumption (ft²)
	Full housing stock	New housing units		
U.S.—full population	1,883	2,123	0.46	992
U.S.—bottom quintile of income distribution	1,416	1,556	0.42	855
France	964	1,218	0.60	402
Germany	964	1,177	0.50	438
United Kingdom	935	890	0.43	407

SOURCES: Figures for the United States were compiled by the authors using microdata from the 2005 American Housing Survey (U.S. Census Bureau 2006b). Data for France, Germany, and the United Kingdom come from National Agency for Enterprise and Housing 2004, tables 2.1, 2.2, 3.1, and 3.7.
NOTES: For the U.S. data, observations without reported incomes were dropped, as were top-coded values, to reduce the sensitivity of the means to outliers. Thus, the numbers in the first row reflect information on both owners and renters in the United States. The second row is based on the subset of those observations with reported incomes in the bottom quintile of the income distribution. The information for the United Kingdom is from 2001; the information for France and Germany is from 2002.

to sampling variation in the AHS, there certainly is no evidence the gap is widening.[3] The rise in housing consumption depicted above is not driven entirely by the increasingly good fortunes of the relatively rich. The living space of poorer owners and renters is larger today than it has been at any time over the past two decades. Despite rising housing prices, poorer Americans are consuming more housing than in the past.

We can also compare American housing with housing in other developed countries. Table 2-1 compares the United States with three major European countries. For U.S. housing consumption, we use the data above from the American Housing Survey, examining the full population as well as those in the bottom quintile of the income distribution. The first column gives the average number of square feet per dwelling for all residences, whether rented or owner occupied. The second column gives the average number of square feet per dwelling for new units. U.S. homes are substantially larger than those in the European countries, and this gap is particularly striking for new construction.

TABLE 2-2

THE DECLINE OF SUBSTANDARD HOUSING IN THE STOCK

Census year	% Units without complete plumbing facilities	% Units without sewer connection or septic tank	Overcrowded housing stock	
			>1 person per room	> 1.5 persons per room
1940	45.3	35.3	20.2	9.0
1950	35.5	24.5	15.7	6.2
1960	16.8	10.3	11.5	3.6
1970	6.9	4.3	8.2	2.2
1980	2.7	1.8	4.5	1.4
1990	1.1	1.1	4.9	2.1
2000	NA	NA	5.7	2.7

SOURCE: U.S. Census Bureau. Decennial Census, Long Form Housing Characteristics. Washington, D.C.: U.S. Census Bureau, 1940–2000.
NOTE: NA means the question about these features was not asked in the 2000 census.

The gap between the U.S. and Europe is also evident on a per capita basis. In the third column, we show the number of people per room in the United States and in Europe. The gaps here are smaller, but this clearly is due to differences in room sizes in European countries versus the United States. In the final column, we compute per capita living space by dividing the square footage per dwelling by the number of people per dwelling for all units. Not only are Americans consuming much more housing than Europeans on average, but even those in the bottom fifth of the U.S. income distribution are living in larger residences than the average resident in major European countries.[4]

Structure size obviously is only one measure of housing quality. Public health concerns and more general worries about substandard housing for the poor once focused on plumbing facilities and crowding. The data in table 2-2 taken from the decennial censuses show that these concerns largely have disappeared. Column one reports on whether the housing unit has complete plumbing facilities, meaning hot and cold piped water, a flush toilet, and a bathtub or shower; barely more than 1 percent of housing units lack these features, according to the most recent data available from 1990. Forty years

TABLE 2-3
HOMEOWNERSHIP RATES (U.S. AVERAGES)

Census year	% Homeowners
1900	46.5
1910	45.9
1920	45.6
1930	47.8
1940	43.6
1950	55.0
1960	61.9
1970	62.9
1980	64.4
1990	64.2
2000	66.2

SOURCE: U.S. Census Bureau. Decennial Census, Housing Characteristics. Washington, D.C.: U.S. Census Bureau, 1900–2000.

ago, one in six units did not have hot water and a flush toilet, and that still was much lower than the nearly one in two units without complete plumbing in 1940, as the nation was recovering from the Great Depression.[5]

There have been similarly dramatic declines in the fraction of units without access to a public sewer or without a septic tank or cesspool. The second column of table 2-2 shows that one in ten units had no such system in 1960, while the number in 1990 was about one in one hundred. While it is now assumed that all housing will include such basic facilities, this was not true even in the recent past. The dramatic reduction in the fraction of very low-quality housing is a major triumph of the postwar economy.[6]

Crowding, as defined by the number of persons per room, also shows dramatic declines over the past sixty years, but there was a trend change in the 1980s. The final two columns in table 2-2 document that over one-tenth of housing units were crowded—that is, had more than one person per room—in 1960. This fell to below 5 percent of all units in 1980, but that fraction has crept up a bit over the past two decades. In 2000, 5.7 percent of all housing units were crowded according to this definition.[7] Essentially, about 95 percent of all homes now have less than one person per room.

The most recent data, from the 2005 American Housing Survey, confirm that substandard housing has become quite rare. This source shows that 1.2 percent of occupied homes lacked some or all plumbing facilities, with 1.6 percent not having a complete kitchen. Crowding in the form of more than one person per room existed in only 2.4 percent of all occupied units according to this sample (U.S. Census Bureau 2006b, fig. 1). This is about one half the share found in the 2000 census. Effectively, between one in seventy-five and one in one hundred units are substandard by the traditional definition. This is not zero, but it does suggest that the problem is much less severe today than it was thirty to forty years ago, when it was a major national issue in our large urban areas and throughout rural America.

Another indication of the overall high quality of the housing stock also comes from the 2005 AHS, which reports that nearly two-thirds of occupied units (62.9 percent) have a dishwasher, 85 percent have air conditioning of some type (including room units, not only central air), and almost all (97.1 percent) have a telephone. Essentially, quality standards have risen so much over the past few decades that to be "substandard" now has more to do with the absence of a dishwasher and air conditioning than with incomplete plumbing or overcrowding.

One further measure of housing consumption involves homeownership rates. At the national level, homeownership rates have been above 60 percent for the last forty years, with the rate increasing by five percentage points since 1960, as shown in table 2-3. There has been some decline in homeownership over the last twenty-four months, but American homeownership still remains high by historical standards. However, these rates are not high everywhere in the country, and they have not been consistently rising in a number of markets. Figure 2-4 plots homeownership rates for three populous cities with high housing costs in each census year since 1950. Homeownership rates in Los Angeles, Boston, and New York are significantly lower than the national average. Moreover, homeownership rates have been trending down in Los Angeles, as more rental units are built.

We do not join those who think that more homeownership always is better.[8] Still, the steady increase in homeownership nationwide indicates that the housing market is making ownership a possibility for a wider spectrum of the American population, which is impressive given that the

FIGURE 2-4

HOMEOWNERSHIP RATES FOR THE NATION AND SELECT CITIES

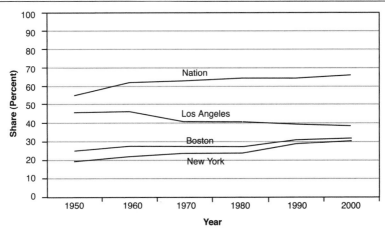

SOURCE: U.S. Census Bureau. Decennial Census, Long Form Housing Characteristics. Washington, D.C.: U.S. Census Bureau, 1950–2000.

typical home is getting bigger and better. That said, there are markets where ownership is less extensive and where there is no trend toward increasing ownership.

House Prices, Incomes, Amenities

While the data on housing consumption seem to offer little that is not good news, the data on housing prices present a much more mixed story. High and rising prices are surely among the most important changes in housing markets over the last thirty years. As we have already argued, high or rising prices are not necessarily a cause for policy concern, nor evidence of an affordability crisis. However, they potentially could be both, so we investigate what might have caused the price appreciation in housing.

Figure 2-5 shows that the overall increase in real house prices has been accompanied by a sharp increase in the dispersion of prices across metropolitan areas. This figure plots the real median house price in constant 2000 dollars since 1950 based on decennial census data for 316 metropolitan

FIGURE 2-5

**GROWING HOUSE-PRICE DISPERSION ACROSS METROPOLITAN AREAS
(AVERAGE VALUES, 316 METRO AREAS)**

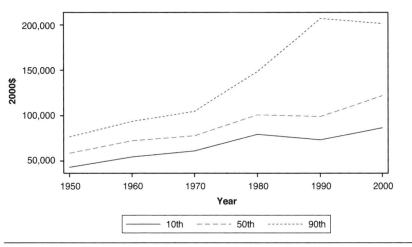

SOURCE: Glaeser, Gyourko, and Saks 2005, figure 1.

areas. House values are presented for the metropolitan areas at the 10th, 50th, and 90th percentiles of the price distribution in each census year. Note that there have been modest increases in real prices at the 10th and 50th percentiles of the distribution, but there has been an enormous increase in prices at the 90th percentile of the distribution. Thus, the average appreciation experienced nationally masks substantial variation across markets. In most metropolitan areas (as evidenced by the plots for the 10th and 50th percentiles), there has been some real price growth, but it has been modest. It is in a relatively few metropolitan areas in the top of the distribution that house prices have shot up, especially since 1970.

If price appreciation has been relatively high in a relatively few markets, then it must be the case that those markets now have very high prices in absolute terms and relative to the rest of the country. Table 2-4 confirms this is the case and identifies the twenty most and least expensive metropolitan areas in the country for housing in 2007 using data on 154 markets collected by the National Association of Realtors. The highest median house prices are found almost exclusively in one of three parts of the country:

TABLE 2-4

**2007 MEDIAN HOUSING PRICES OF EXISTING
SINGLE-FAMILY HOMES IN METROPOLITAN AREAS**

20 Most and Least Expensive Markets in the Country

	Metropolitan statistical area	Median sales price ($1000s)
1	San Jose-Sunnyvale-Santa Clara, CA	836.8
2	San Francisco-Oakland-Fremont, CA	805.4
3	Anaheim-Santa Ana, CA (Orange Co.)	699.6
4	Honolulu, HI	643.5
5	Los Angeles-Long Beach-Santa Ana, CA	589.2
6	San Diego-Carlsbad-San Marcos, CA	588.7
7	New York-Wayne-White Plains, NY-NJ	540.3
8	Bridgeport-Stamford-Norwalk, CT	486.6
9	NY: Nassau-Suffolk, NY	477.2
10	New York-Northern New Jersey-Long Island, NY-NJ-PA	469.7
11	NY: Newark-Union, NJ-PA	443.7
12	Washington-Arlington-Alexandria, DC-VA-MD-WV	430.8
13	Boston-Cambridge-Quincy, MA-NH	395.6
14	Seattle-Tacoma-Bellevue, WA	386.9
15	Barnstable Town, MA	384.7
16	Riverside-San Bernardino-Ontario, CA	381.4
17	NY: Edison, NJ	380.3
18	Boulder, CO	376.2
19	Miami-Fort Lauderdale-Miami Beach, FL	365.5
20	Sacramento—Arden-Arcade—Roseville, CA	342.7

135	Amarillo, TX	118.4
136	Rochester, NY	117.9
137	Dayton, OH	115.6
138	Wichita, KS	115.6
139	Waterloo/Cedar Falls, IA	112.8
140	Topeka, KS	111.9
141	Binghamton, NY	111.1
142	Canton-Massillon, OH	110.3
143	Cumberland, MD-WV	109.4
144	Springfield, IL	109.0

continued on next page

Table 2-4 continued

	Metropolitan statistical area	Median sales price ($1000s)
145	Davenport-Moline-Rock Island, IA-IL	108.7
146	Toledo, OH	106.6
147	Buffalo-Niagara Falls, NY	104.0
148	Erie, PA	98.1
149	Ft. Wayne, IN	97.1
150	South Bend-Mishawaka, IN	90.7
151	Decatur, IL	83.1
152	Saginaw-Saginaw Township North, MI	82.1
153	Elmira, NY	81.6
154	Youngstown-Warren-Boardman, OH-PA	78.9

Source: National Association of Realtors. Metropolitan Median Prices. Washington, D.C.: National Association of Realtors, 2007. http://www.realtor.org/research/research/ metroprice.

(a) coastal California; (b) the Washington, D.C.–New York–Boston corridor; and (c) south Florida. The lowest median house prices are spread throughout the South and Midwest and are found as well in quite a few Rustbelt cities. The range of prices is enormous, running from around $80,000 to over $800,000. This tenfold difference in prices between the top and bottom markets is historically unprecedented.

It is worthwhile to have data on housing prices, but for many policy questions, knowing the user cost of housing is more important. Unfortunately, perfect data on user costs, which depend on the house's price, interest costs, maintenance costs, property taxes, and expected appreciation—and which should also correct for differences in the quality of homes across markets and over time—do not exist. Sales prices or values reported in the decennial census give a good sense of those costs, however, and we will also augment price information with information on rents.

Figure 2-6 reports the time path of rents in the nation's larger cities (defined as those with populations of at least one hundred thousand as of the year 2000). Real rents have increased everywhere, partially because of increasing unit quality. Dispersion in rents across markets is wider now, too, but there is much less divergence between the 10th and 90th percentiles than there is in housing prices. As with house prices, there is a growing

FIGURE 2-6

REAL RENTS, 1950–2000

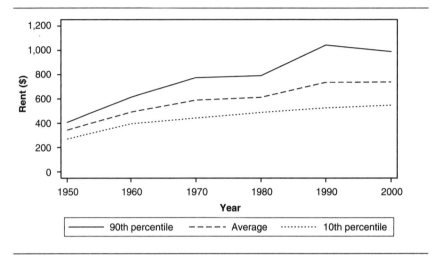

SOURCE: U.S. Census Bureau. *County and City Data Book.* Washington, D.C.: U.S. Census Bureau, 1950–2000.
NOTE: Median gross monthly rent of U.S. cities (in 2005 dollars calculated using 254 cities with population of 100,000 or more).

FIGURE 2-7

RENT AS SHARE OF GDP PER CAPITA

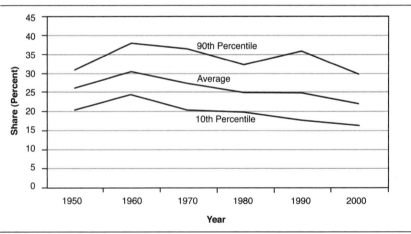

SOURCE: U.S. Census Bureau. *County and City Data Book.* Washington, D.C.: U.S. Census Bureau, 1950–2000; author's calculations from the U.S. Census Bureau, *County and City Data Book.*
NOTE: Median gross rent of U.S. cities as percentage of national GDP per capita (in 2005 dollars, calculated using 254 cities with population of 100,000 or more).

FIGURE 2-8

COUNTY-LEVEL HOUSE PRICE MAP OF THE CONTINENTAL UNITED STATES

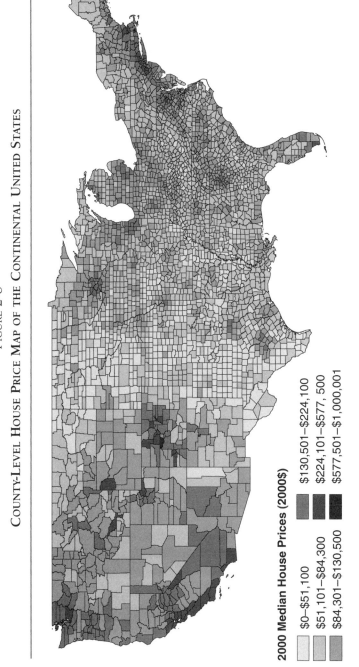

2000 Median House Prices (2000$)

$0–$51,100

$51,101–$84,300

$84,301–$130,500

$130,501–$224,100

$224,101–$577,500

$577,501–$1,000,001

SOURCE: U.S. Census Bureau. 2000 Decennial Census, County Housing Characteristics. Washington, D.C.: U.S. Census Bureau, 2000.

FIGURE 2-9

HOUSE PRICES AND REAL INCOMES

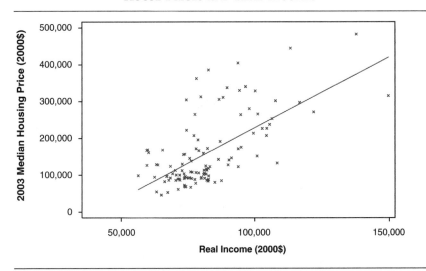

SOURCES: U.S. Census Bureau. 2000 Decennial Census, County Housing Characteristics. Washington, D.C.: U.S. Census Bureau, 2000; Office of Federal Housing Enterprise Oversight. Repeat Sales House Price Index. Washington, D.C.: U.S. Census Bureau, 1993–2008; Bureau of Economic Analysis. State and Local Area Personal Income. Washington, D.C.: Bureau of Economic Analysis, 2003.

dispersion in rents across markets, but the change is not nearly as large, and it moderated more in the 1990s. Moreover, as figure 2-7 documents, rents have been declining relative to national income per capita even in the places where they are the highest and have been growing most rapidly. This suggests that any affordability problems for the typical (i.e., nonpoor) household are unlikely to be associated with renting, and if they do exist will be associated with owner-occupancy.

Figure 2-8 presents a map of the continental United States based on median housing prices by county in 2000 (the last census year available). While absolute conditions have changed since then, the underlying geographic pattern remains. The United States has three basic housing regions. First, there are the truly expensive areas, generally on the coasts. Second, there is the overwhelming majority of counties within the United States, where housing prices hover around $120,000, the national median housing price. Finally, there is a third set of counties where housing prices are significantly below this level. In these places, which are in economic decline,

FIGURE 2-10
HOUSE PRICES AND WEATHER

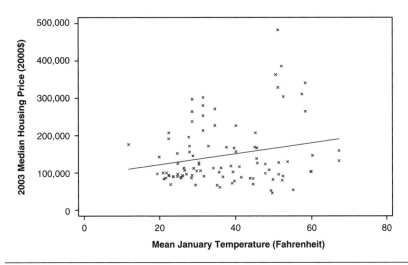

SOURCES: U.S. Census Bureau. 2000 Decennial Census, County Housing Characteristics. Washington, D.C.: U.S. Census Bureau, 2000; Office of Federal Housing Enterprise Oversight. Repeat Sales House Price Index. Washington, D.C.: Office of Federal Housing Enterprise Oversight, 1993–2008; United States National Climatic Data Center. U.S. Climate Normals 1971–2000. Washington, D.C.: U.S. National Climatic Data Center, 1971–2000.

housing prices are often substantially below the cost of new construction (Glaeser and Gyourko 2005).

The divergence in housing prices may be unprecedented, but these differences across metropolitan areas are not random. Standard urban economics tells us that they reflect different economic conditions (e.g., differential productivity of firm clusters across markets) and different amenities (e.g., weather). Thus, San Francisco should be relatively expensive because it combines extremely high wages with an extremely benign climate.

That high incomes and a favorable climate are, indeed, associated with higher house prices is confirmed in figures 2-9 and 2-10. Figure 2-9 illustrates the very strong relationship between income and housing prices across metropolitan areas using data for the year 2003.[9] Not surprisingly, people are richer in places that are more expensive. Just over 50 percent of the variation in housing price across areas is associated with variation in income across areas. The relationship of house prices to the weather is less strong but still quite visible in figure 2-10.[10] Warm places are attractive to people and tend to have higher prices.

Thus, high housing prices in some metropolitan areas can be understood as the result of robust labor markets and good amenities. People are getting something (e.g., high wages and nice weather) in return for those high prices, but there are certain instances in which these prices may be a cause for concern. First, there are people within even the richest metropolitan area who will have trouble paying for their housing. Moreover, high housing prices do not solely reflect demand but can be manifestations of restrictions on supply. If the supply of housing is the result of some sort of market failure, perhaps created by the government itself, then this is just the sort of problem that good policy could be working to fix.

We have already indicated our view that the presence of low-income people in areas with high house prices does not necessitate a housing policy response. There may be a case for increased government aid to poor people in high-cost areas, although even that is debatable since those high costs are often offset by other benefits (Glaeser 1998). Moreover, artificially reducing housing costs in expensive areas will reduce the incentives for people to respond to prices by moving, and removing those incentives is a mistake. We should want people to respond to market signals and move to places where incomes and productivity are high, or where costs are low. Even if high prices call for more aid, they do not imply the need for intervention in the local housing market unless there is evidence of a market failure. If housing prices, no matter how high, simply reflect strong demand and normal supply conditions, then it is hard to see why a policy intervention is called for.

However, if these high prices reflect something less benign in the housing market, then the case for government intervention becomes stronger. Thus, it is particularly important to understand whether these high prices are also reflecting some sort of market failure in the supply of housing. We turn to that issue now.

Housing Prices and Construction Costs

High prices always and everywhere reflect the intersection of strong demand and limited supply. If demand for a product is weak, then prices

FIGURE 2-11
HOUSE PRICES AND NEW CONSTRUCTION

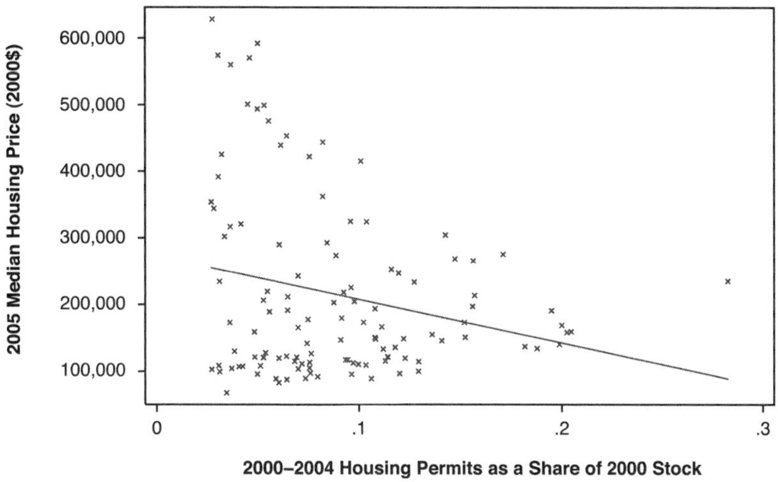

2000–2004 Housing Permits as a Share of 2000 Stock

SOURCES: Office of Federal Housing Enterprise Oversight. Repeat Sales House Price Index. Washington, D.C.: Office of Federal Housing Enterprise Oversight, 1993–2008; U.S. Census Bureau. 2000 Decennial Census, County Housing Characteristics. Washington, D.C.: U.S. Census Bureau, 2000; U.S. Census Bureau Manufacturing, Mining and Construction Statistics. County Building Permits 2000–2004. Washington, D.C.: U.S. Census Bureau, 2000–2004.

cannot be high, no matter how tight supply may be. If supply is unrestricted, then prices cannot rise much above production costs, no matter how strong demand may be. These basic principles of microeconomics apply to housing, just as they do to all goods.

While differences in income across markets certainly influence the demand for housing, there is abundant evidence that price differences across space don't just reflect differences in demand. Supply also matters. Figure 2-11 graphs house prices in 2005 against the share of the housing stock added over the previous five years. If demand for housing was the only thing that differed across markets, then we should expect to see abundant new construction accompany high prices. If supply conditions were the same across markets, then high prices which reflect strong demand should elicit a robust supply response, and low prices should leave new construction in the doldrums.

FIGURE 2-12

MANHATTAN PRICES AND PERMITS

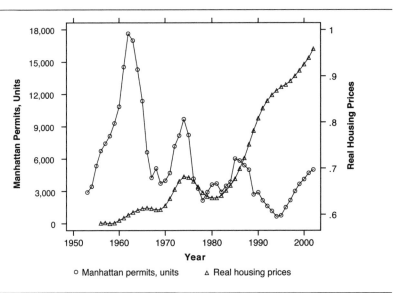

SOURCE: Glaeser, Gyourko, and Saks 2005, figure 1.
NOTES: Both the Manhattan housing permit and price series are four-year moving averages. Building permits are combined single-family and multi-family permits for Manhattan (New York County). The real housing price series is the NY-NJ-LI metropolitan area Consumer Price Index for shelter, deflated by the gross domestic product deflator from the National Income and Product Accounts (rescaled to equal 1 in 2002).

However, figure 2-11 does not depict a positive relationship between price and new construction, which would be the case if the supply of housing was the same everywhere. The steeply negative slope in the picture indicates that areas with high house prices such as San Francisco, Santa Barbara, and New York have experienced very little increase in their housing stocks. In contrast, metropolitan areas that saw substantial new construction (as a share of their 2000 housing stock), such as Las Vegas, Phoenix, and Orlando, have lower prices. We cannot understand why some places have high prices and little construction while others have abundant construction and moderate prices without accepting that supply conditions differ across space.

Data over time for the same markets also suggest that supply-side conditions help account for high prices in some markets. Figure 2-12, which is taken from Glaeser, Gyourko, and Saks (2005), plots series on prices and

FIGURE 2-13
REAL CONSTRUCTION COSTS OVER TIME

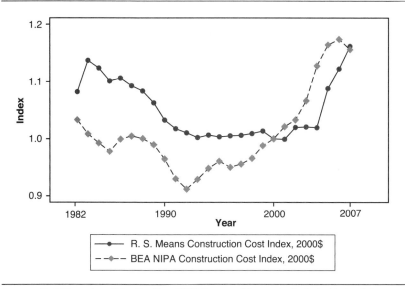

SOURCES: *R. S. Means Assemblies Cost Data 2008*; Bureau of Economic Analysis, National Income and Product Accounts, Residential Construction Cost Index.

new construction in New York City. Besides documenting that Manhattan had much higher permitting levels in the 1960s than today, the figure indicates that booming prices on the island since 1980 have not been accompanied by a rise in the number of new units. If all changes were driven by rising demand, then we should expect to see increases in prices accompanied by increases in permitting, but we see no change, or even a slight decline, in permitting when prices rise in this market.

In sum, the data suggest that high and rising prices, particularly in America's coastal markets, are the result of rising demand coming together with restricted supply. This conclusion is reinforced by the fact that construction costs cannot account for much of the price increase in these markets. Figure 2-13 reports aggregate national data on real construction costs from two different data sources—the federal government and a private-sector consultant to the homebuilding industry. These series are each indexed to have a value of one in the year 2000. Even with the very large increases in

TABLE 2-5

2007 CONSTRUCTION COSTS IN MARKETS WITH 1 MILLION+ PEOPLE

		Economy unit cost per sq.ft. (2007$)
1	New York	$85.33
2	San Francisco	$79.74
3	Boston-Worcester-Lawrence-Lowell-Brockton	$76.05
4	Philadelphia	$74.71
5	Chicago	$73.95
6	Newark	$73.44
7	Minneapolis-St. Paul	$73.16
8	Bergen-Passaic	$72.68
9	Hartford	$71.22
10	New Haven-Bridgeport-Stamford-Danbury-Waterbury	$71.18
11	Sacramento	$71.02
12	Los Angeles-Long Beach	$70.38
13	Orange County	$69.43
14	Riverside-San Bernardino	$69.27
15	San Diego	$68.84
16	Detroit	$68.56
17	Seattle-Bellevue-Everett	$67.97
18	St. Louis	$67.65
19	Portland-Vancouver	$67.21
20	Kansas City	$67.01
21	Milwaukee-Waukesha	$66.97
22	Buffalo-Niagara-Falls	$66.86
23	Las Vegas	$66.10
24	Cleveland-Lorain-Elyria	$65.39
25	Rochester	$64.83
26	Pittsburgh	$64.71
27	Columbus	$61.50
28	Indianapolis	$61.11
29	Baltimore	$60.47
30	Cincinnati	$60.43
31	Tampa-St. Petersburg-Clearwater	$60.27
32	Louisville	$59.84
33	Miami	$59.04

continued on next page

Table 2-5 continued

		Economy unit cost per sq.ft. (2007$)
34	Orlando	$58.73
35	Atlanta	$58.69
36	Phoenix-Mesa	$58.57
37	Richmond-Petersburg	$58.41
38	Norfolk-Virginia Beach-Newport News	$57.97
39	Houston	$57.89
40	Fort Lauderdale	$57.74
41	New Orleans	$57.58
42	Salt Lake City-Ogden	$57.34
43	Nashville	$57.26
44	Memphis	$56.74
45	Jacksonville	$55.12
46	Dallas	$54.96
47	Grand Rapids-Muskegon-Holland	$54.40
48	San Antonio	$54.09
49	Oklahoma City	$53.77
50	Fort Worth-Arlington	$53.45
51	Charlotte-Gastonia-Rock Hill	$52.66
52	Raleigh-Durham-Chapel Hill	$52.38
53	Greensboro-Winston-Salem-High Point	$52.22
54	Austin-San Marcos	$52.18

SOURCE: R. S. Means 2008.

construction costs over the past few years, in real terms these costs still are not appreciably different from what they were in 1980.[11]

There is variation in construction costs across markets. Table 2-5 shows that a single-family house of modest quality can be built for under $80 per square foot (in 2007 dollars) in almost any major metropolitan area in the country. These data use cost estimates for the year 2007 from the R. S. Means Company and are for a 2,000 ft² dwelling that just meets all code requirements in each metropolitan area. The highest physical construction cost is only $170,660 in the New York market ($170,660 = $85.33 per square foot × 2,000 ft² home).

TABLE 2-6

RATIOS OF PRICE TO CONSTRUCTION COST OVER TIME

	Ratios of price to construction cost (P/CC) over time 102 metropolitan areas					
	1950	1960	1970	1980	1990	2000
Mean	0.83	0.90	0.88	1.15	1.35	1.46
Standard deviation	0.16	0.16	0.16	0.30	0.59	0.55
90th percentile	1.04	1.10	1.12	1.49	2.17	1.85
Maximum	1.19	1.30	1.31	2.17	3.49	4.06
	Implied land share ($\sim 1 - CC/P$)					
90th percentile	0.04	0.09	0.11	0.33	0.54	0.46
Maximum	0.16	0.23	0.24	0.54	0.71	0.75

SOURCE: Glaeser, Gyourko, and Saks 2005, table 2.
NOTES: Mean house prices are constructed for each metropolitan area using county-level data from the relevant decennial census. Construction cost data are from various years of R. S. Means, *Assemblies Cost Data*. See Glaeser, Gyourko, and Saks (2005) for more detail.

Given that we know total house prices are far higher in high-cost markets, this finding indicates that other factors, such as high land values, must constrain developers from supplying substantially more units in these markets. Table 2-6 confirms that this is, indeed, the case. These data, which are taken from Glaeser, Gyourko, and Saks (2005), report the ratio of price to construction costs for 102 major metropolitan areas over the past half century. Taken literally, a ratio of 1 would imply that land is free, as house price equals construction costs. Note that the average ratio does not go above 1 until 1980, and it has increased sharply since then. In the latest census year, the typical ratio of house price to construction cost is 1.46 to 1. It is 1.85 to 1 for the top 10 percent of metropolitan areas, and is extraordinarily high (above 4) in one case.

We refer to the share of price that is not explained by construction costs as the "land share." This term actually includes not only the cost of land in the area but all other nonconstruction costs in producing new housing as well. Implied land shares are listed in the bottom panel of table 2-6. In 10 percent of our metropolitan areas, the share of land value in total house price is at least 46 percent. This highlights the fact that it is prices, not construction costs, that have risen more in our most expensive housing markets.

However, that still does not tell us what is responsible for these changes. The appropriate policy response (which includes no intervention as an option) hinges on the answer to that question. One potential explanation is that these primarily coastal markets literally are running out of land. After all, they have an ocean on one border and are land-constrained in that sense. In this case, high prices would be due to strong demand for the amenities and productivity of these coastal markets combined with a natural supply constraint. Land would be fundamentally, not artificially, scarce, and its high price would reflect its scarcity value. If so, there would be no legitimate economic justification for government intervention to lower prices, even though house values are well above construction costs, because high land values are needed to efficiently ration scarce sites in these markets.

Another plausible explanation is that the land scarcity is not the result of innate shortages, but rather of the limits created by land-use regulation. According to this view, there is available developable land (on which one could build up, not just horizontally), but regulation prevents its development. This scarcity is artificial in the sense that policy created it. If local policy is primarily responsible for the wide and growing gap between house prices and construction costs in many of the nation's coastal markets, then housing in those areas is unnecessarily, and possibly inefficiently, expensive.

If the local land-use regulations that restrict supply are accurately reflecting real externalities, such as greater congestion or pollution, associated with new construction in particular areas, then their impact on prices and construction may be efficient. If, on the other hand, these regulations reflect more the ability of local homeowners to organize and less any real negative construction externalities, then they may be quite inefficient. In that case, there may be a sound rationale for public policy to help lower prices by increasing supply.

3

Public Intervention in U.S. Housing Markets—A Historical Perspective

The housing market long has been subject to a wide range of government policies. Even before there was a United States, our localities were setting down rules that governed building. Over the course of the twentieth century, those rules have become more stringent and have been joined by many other government interventions, some at the local and some at the national level. We must study these policies if we are to understand the current state of housing in America and if we are to introduce new policies that are sound and respect the diversity of market conditions that exist across the country.

This chapter offers a historical overview of American housing policy since its inception and looks specifically at the primary rationales for government intervention in the housing markets. Chapters 4 and 5 go on to analyze the policies that are most important today.

Housing Regulation and Externalities

The earliest instances of government housing policy in America seem to have been associated with threat of fire. Given the extensive damage created by the great Chicago fire, we shouldn't be surprised that governments sought to reduce the threat of such disasters. Novak (1996) describes how local governments in the nineteenth century restricted building materials and regulated new construction to make the spread of fire more difficult.

A person building his own home might not take into account the harm that a fire-prone house could cause his neighbors. That harm is a good illustration of what economists call a negative externality, which can justify some type of government intervention. Of course, just because there is a case for government intervention does not mean that all interventions actually are justifiable. So one can reasonably question the need for St. Louis's ordinance of 1849, which banned all wooden construction. However, it is clear that there can be externalities requiring regulatory intervention by local governments.

Over the course of the late nineteenth century, concerns about public health arose to complement concerns about fire in the regulation of housing. The early public health concerns about housing were voiced by those such as England's Edwin Chadwick. Chadwick mistakenly believed in the miasma theory, which held that diseases such as cholera were airborne and more likely to spread in dense dwellings. The ultimate discovery that cholera and similar urban scourges were waterborne helped push cities, in the United States and elsewhere, to invest heavily in water and sewage systems (Cutler and Miller 2006). Still, the interest in improving sanitary conditions within the home did not disappear, as muckraking journalists such as the famous photographer and author Jacob Riis focused public attention on the low quality of urban tenements.

New York's Tenement House Act of 1901, which followed a less effective tenement act passed in 1867, began the process of imposing strict rules on unit quality. The 1901 legislation barred the construction of dumbbell units and required a toilet for each tenement (Von Hoffman 1998). The attention to air flow led to a requirement for two windows in every tenement, one to the outside and the other to the indoor courtyard. The 1901 Tenement Act became a model that was copied by many other cities throughout the country. In a sense, it set the stage for zoning codes such as the Zoning Resolution of 1916 that would soon follow.

New York's 1916 zoning ordinance was also motivated by concern over health externalities, but in addition it pointed the way toward the greater attention that would be paid to aesthetic issues in the future. The ordinance banned from residential districts some particularly noxious commercial activities that residents were likely to consider aesthetic annoyances, not merely health-related externalities. It advanced height and setback regulations meant to bring more air and light into the city, again for reasons having to do not only with health but with aesthetics; the fact that new buildings block sight lines is an obvious aesthetic externality. Over time, zoning and other land-use controls grew to address any new development that imposed any costs—of whatever form—on existing neighbors.

Glaeser, Schuetz, and Ward (2006) illustrate this point in describing the vast array of land-use regulations currently in place in the Boston area. Some of these regulations, such as rules regarding septic systems, are rooted in typical public health concerns. However, the septic restrictions are both so random and so draconian that it is hard to imagine that they serve only health-related purposes. Similarly, wetlands regulations play a potentially important role protecting the ecosystem, but in practice, these regulations rely on vague definitions of "wetlands," and the variation across districts is enormous. Other regulations in Boston concern sidewalk width within subdivisions, minimum lot sizes, and lot shapes (which must be sufficiently uniform).

These zoning regulations, and the many like them that exist throughout the country, are best understood as reflecting a desire to limit, or stop completely, any new construction that imposes some form of externality on existing homeowners. While there is little doubt that such externalities do exist, it is far from clear that these rules are appropriately designed to address them.

Two classes of externalities that seem particularly important in current land-use debates are congestion externalities and environmental externalities. Congestion externalities occur when a new house implies more drivers in the area. Those drivers impose an externality on others by slowing traffic on the road as well as causing congestion in public services like schools, where new residents overload teachers. Of course, new construction would not create these externalities if tax payments were sufficient to cover the social costs of increased driving or use of public facilities. More generally, the existence of congestion externalities provides a case for imposing an appropriate congestion tax on drivers, or even an appropriate tax on new development, but it does not justify any and every zoning rule meant to slow down new building.

Environmental externalities occur when new development eliminates open land or forest that either had been directly enjoyed by other residents or had played some important part in the ecosystem. Assuming this land was privately owned, it is more appropriate to discuss the positive externalities created by the old uses rather than the negative externalities created by the new uses, as the presumption should not be that privately owned land will remain undeveloped.

Environmental concerns can be entirely and obviously local in character—citizens like to play on a particular open field—or be rooted in more global concerns. The opponents of sprawl, for example, argue that unfettered development presents a great challenge to the American environment, both directly in its elimination of open space, and indirectly by encouraging greater energy use that promotes global warming. However, even if new development causes environmental damage to the planet as a whole, it does not follow that local regulation of that development is an appropriate response. After all, local land-use restrictions may not reduce the overall level of development in the country, which is closely tied to the overall level of new household formation. Instead, local land-use restrictions may just push development somewhere else, particularly to where there are no neighbors to object.

If regulation does push development out to less populated areas, the net environmental impact could be negligible or even negative. For example, one can reasonably argue that the antigrowth movement in California did little to reduce the amount of sprawl in the country as a whole, but just moved it away from older areas to the urban fringe, and away from California to Nevada and Arizona. Since there is little reason to think that building in less developed areas is desirable from an environmental perspective, local environmentalism could be counterproductive nationally.

A final externality that has played a major role in the debates about housing policy is "citizenship." For decades, people have argued that homeowners make better citizens, which in practical terms means that they provide positive externalities for their neighbors by improving the quality of government or the quality of life in the neighborhood. Because homeowners have a financial stake in the community and they move less often, the argument goes, they have greater incentives to invest in improving their localities.

But the evidence on the positive spillovers from homeownership is ambiguous, and subsidizing homeownership to achieve these benefits may not pay off. There is little doubt that homeowners are in fact more likely to vote, to be knowledgeable about local officials, and to say that they work to solve local problems (DiPasquale and Glaeser 1999). However, these effects may reflect the fact that a certain type of person becomes a homeowner to begin with, and results from empirical analyses that look at people over time are ambiguous. Thus, research has not yet managed to quantify any truly convincing positive externalities that may derive from homeownership.

Correcting Market Failures

Housing market interventions have also been seen as a needed response to uncompetitive features of certain markets. Specifically, some have argued that landlords or developers hold a degree of market power and that regulation is needed to protect consumers, but we believe that these arguments are not tenable.

The extremely large number of homebuilders nationwide certainly makes the construction industry look competitive. The 1997 Economic Census reports almost 140,000 firms in the single-family construction business. There is concentration in the industry, but it is not dominated by only a handful of companies, as there were over seventeen hundred firms with revenues in excess of $10 million annually. There are many fewer builders of apartment complexes, but the same data source indicates over seventy-five hundred firms in the sector. At least for big cities such as New York, there is no evidence of control by a few firms. Glaeser, Gyourko, and Saks (2005) document that there were over 100 multifamily builders headquartered in Manhattan alone, with another 329 in the rest of the city. There has been growth in the number of large developers in recent years, but this change likely is a response to an increasingly complex regulatory environment that creates a need for large legal and planning departments to fight the challenges to development. At least at the metropolitan area level, the data indicate that there are plenty of suppliers of housing.

In the case of the rental market, some distinguished economists (Arnott 1995) have suggested that the heterogeneous nature of the housing market gives landlords some degree of market power. This viewpoint argues that a rental market is comprised not by the city itself, but rather by a small subset of buildings within that city which offer roughly similar apartments in roughly similar neighborhoods. But it is hard to see how landlords have any market power before a tenant moves into an apartment in any larger city. In any reasonably sized market, there are at least five or six landlords offering roughly comparable apartments to most prospective tenants at any given time.

Another view is that once a tenant moves into an apartment, the landlord can exploit him by precipitously raising rents, since high moving costs render renters somewhat immobile once they have moved into their unit. So-called second-generation rent controls are meant to limit the ability of landlords to raise rents and thereby limit the possibility of this *ex post* rent extraction (Arnott 1995). Of course, since landlords as well as tenants face costs if the tenant moves, it is also possible for tenants to hold up landlords. Moreover, there is nothing to stop tenants and landlords from signing multiyear leases that could address this problem without rent control or other regulatory intervention.

From our perspective, a much more serious market failure involves the real estate brokerage business, where multiple listing services seem to restrict competition among real estate agents. The 6 percent commissions paid to agents are much higher than in other nations, and it is hard to see how the commission structure reflects differences in the marginal cost of selling different homes. A $1,000,000 home is unlikely to require five times more effort to sell than a $200,000 dollar home. Hsieh and Moretti (2003) provide evidence showing that the combination of fixed commissions and free entry into the real estate industry seems to create social waste.

Many of the largest interventions in the housing market have been undertaken to prevent alleged failures in the credit market. For example, the original impetus for Federal Housing Administration (FHA) mortgage insurance seems to have been a belief that there was a market failure in the mortgage industry. Prior to 1934, most mortgages were short term, and during the Great Depression there were many foreclosures, which helped keep housing prices low. The supporters of federal mortgage insurance thought that insecure mortgages were part of the bank-run problem that led to insecurity in the banking industry and limited growth of the mortgage industry. They saw mortgage insurance as a tool against runs in the mortgage industry. Banks that sense trouble want to foreclose quickly on their housing loans in order to get the homes before the housing market collapses. But if all banks foreclose at once, this will only hasten the housing market collapse. Mortgage insurance reduces the incentive for banks to rush to foreclose and hence staves off market failure.

Another justification for mortgage insurance emphasizes a potential adverse selection problem in the mortgage market. If lenders lack information on borrowers, and if only the borrowers with the greatest risks apply for mortgages, then the entire market may break down. Mortgage insurance helps to ensure that banks are willing to lend to a wider spectrum of the population by lessening the risk they undertake in doing so.

We have limited sympathy for these arguments, but it is hard to argue with the success of the mortgage market in the postwar era. Little is to be gained by debating whether the FHA was a reasonable intervention over seventy years ago. A more reasonable argument exists over the current need for government mortgage insurance, or more importantly the need for ongoing government subsidization of Freddie Mac and Fannie Mae, given the systemic risks those entities clearly create for the financial system (Glaeser and Jaffee 2006). We briefly address this issue in chapter 5.

In-Kind Redistribution

The final justification for housing policy is to use housing subsidies as a form of in-kind redistribution. Economists generally prefer pure income redistribution to redistribution in-kind. After all, giving poor people goods instead of cash just acts to limit their options. If we are trying to help the poor as much as possible, and if we assume that they are the best judges of their own needs, then we should presumably want to give them as much choice as possible about what to consume. A standard exercise in undergraduate economics shows that an in-kind transfer generates less welfare for the recipient than an equal transfer of cash.

There are three responses to the case against in-kind redistribution. First, paternalists argue that the poor do not know what is good for them and will spend transfers on things that do not improve their welfare. This viewpoint has been given new strength by advances in behavioral economics that suggest people do not always act in their self-interest. For example, if people lacked self-control and were prone to "hyperbolic discounting"—that is, tended to prefer a smaller benefit sooner to a much larger benefit later (Laibson 1997)—then they might prefer being given durable goods like housing rather than an equivalent sum of cash. Yet why should public employees be in a position to make decisions for the poor? They may be subject to the same biases, and certainly know less about the subsidy recipients than the recipients themselves. We therefore have little sympathy for the view that private individuals are well served by having governments make their consumption decisions for them.

However, there are two other justifications for in-kind redistribution that we find more compelling. The first emphasizes the desires of taxpayers rather than the benefits for recipients of redistribution. According to this view, the preference of the taxpaying population that the poor be relieved of specific wants trumps the right of the poor to make their own consumption decisions. This is the rationale behind such programs as food stamps and Medicaid. A welfare recipient might prefer to use a cash transfer on a trip, but taxpayers prefer to see the recipient well fed or healthy rather than enjoying a weekend in Las Vegas. Housing may be similar to health and nutrition, and many—including Franklin Roosevelt and John F. Kennedy—have argued that it is unacceptable for the poor to live in substandard housing, whether they might choose to or not. One component of housing policy, then, is an attempt to make sure that poor people consume more housing. In-kind transfers thus serve not only to make the recipient better off, but also to meet the wishes of the donors.

Perhaps homelessness is the most obvious example of a problem taxpayers want to address with in-kind benefits rather than cash transfers. It seems clear that well-off taxpayers view homelessness as a terrible thing, while some homeless people prefer living on the streets to making the sacrifices required to live in a shelter. Giving unrestricted financial aid to these homeless people might increase their well-being, but in at least some cases it would not move them into housing units, and it would not have the same benefits for middle-class taxpayers as a policy that was focused exclusively on getting the homeless off the streets.

A second rationale for in-kind redistribution is to ensure that benefits intended for children actually go to help them. Transfers to poorer households are controlled by parents, who (even if they are altruistic toward their children) may choose to spend only part of this income on their children. In-kind transfers provide a way of making sure that government aid goes toward spending that directly benefits children. Public education and preschool programs such as Head Start are obvious models of in-kind redistribution that are meant to bypass parents and provide transfers directly to children. Food stamps and Medicaid also serve in part to provide basic nutrition and health care for children.

Housing policy, too, can be justified as a means of providing basic commodities for children. If we believe that children benefit from having a healthier or larger home or a home in a better neighborhood, then housing transfers can be a way of taking care of children. Green and White (1997) have shown that the children of homeowners are much more successful than the children of renters, but this work (like DiPasquale and Glaeser 1999) lacks an experimental component that could convincingly demonstrate that this is more than mere correlation. Certainly, the thought of children growing up in unsanitary, crowded conditions was one early justification for state intervention in housing markets.

Housing policy aimed at improving housing consumption for poorer children can intend to improve either structure or neighborhood or both. While inadequate structure may have been the main concern of reformers in the Progressive Era, today housing advocates are at least as interested in the ability of housing policy to racially integrate housing markets and to enable poor people to grow up with more successful peers and role models. In the forty years since the Coleman report (1966), social scientists have generally concurred with its view that peers are important both in schools and neighborhoods. This has lent some support to the view that housing policy should help poorer families move into richer neighborhoods. While we have considerable sympathy for this view, the Moving-To-Opportunity experiment, recently analyzed by Katz, Kling, and Liebman (2007), throws some cold water on this argument by showing only modest social and economic gains for children whose families receive housing vouchers that enable them to move to a better neighborhood.

In sum, in-kind transfers to enable greater consumption of housing by the poor can be justified even without paternalism. However, we do not believe there is an overwhelming case for directly subsidizing housing for the poor rather than providing them cash.

Conclusion

The history of government intervention in housing markets offers two primary rationales for such action. The first rests on the existence of some inefficiency in the market that requires public policy to correct it. The second involves a desire for redistribution to individuals deemed deserving by society. However, the fact that we have conceptually sound justifications for intervention does not mean that current policies themselves are sound. The more detailed analysis of current policies in the next two chapters—of direct interventions that control price and quantity in chapter 4 and indirect interventions through the tax code and implicit subsidies in chapter 5—shows that almost all existing policy is misguided and, in some cases, counterproductive in terms of making housing more affordable.

4

Current Policies—Price and Quantity Controls

Housing regulations that directly control prices or quantities tend not to involve the vast government expenditures associated with housing tax breaks and housing subsidies; but they have probably had a more important impact on housing markets.

Price and quantity regulations have historically been motivated by different factors. Price regulations have almost always been a response to some sort of concern for equity. Quantity regulations generally are justified on the basis of an alleged externality. While suburban land-use regulation and Manhattan rent control are rarely linked, they both represent a very direct attempt by the government to control some aspect of the housing market. These direct controls often are extremely effective, but their power means that they also have a great capacity to harm housing markets if they are poorly designed or fundamentally misguided. Our view is that the track record of price controls is almost universally negative, and that the track record of land-use regulations is, at best, mixed. There clearly are external effects of new development that warrant some sensible regulation, but many localities have responded to them by severely limiting building per se.

Price Controls

Rent control historically has been among the most important interventions in housing markets. The original American rent controls were imposed following the Emergency Price Control Act of 1942 during the Second World War. Later, rents effectively were frozen at their levels in March of 1943. The

58

act expired in 1947 and was replaced with the Federal Housing and Rent Act of 1947. This legislation eliminated rent control on buildings built after 1947 and effectively turned rent control over to the states.

Fortunately, rent control has fallen out of favor, almost certainly because it has failed to achieve its main goal of making housing generally more affordable in high-cost markets. Today, thirty-two states ban their municipalities from enacting local rent-control rules.[1] There are now only four states in the United States with rent-controlled cities: California, Maryland, New York, and New Jersey.

There have been two basic types of rent control in the United States. One, which still exists in New York City and Santa Monica, has capped rents at a level far below current market rates for those tenants who have lived in their apartments for a long time. Those rent levels would not persist if these tenants moved. The other type, often referred to as rent stabilization and seen in New York, Newark, Santa Monica, and Washington, allows landlords and tenants to fix rents more or less freely when the tenants first occupy the apartment, but limits increases thereafter.

Research on New York City's controls confirms that rents are lower for those able to occupy controlled units. According to data from the 1999 New York City Housing and Vacancy Survey analyzed by Glaeser and Luttmer (2003), the mean monthly rent paid for controlled units was $462, versus $820 for rent-stabilized units and $1,077 for uncontrolled apartments. While these averages do not adequately control for apartment quality and location, the tendency of current tenants to fight tenaciously for rent-controlled units suggests that they are benefiting from these lower rents. Another piece of evidence that rent control lowers rents is that people in rent-controlled or rent-stabilized units are less likely to change apartments. Thus rent control does make rents lower for current residents of controlled units, but this comes at a very high cost, as we discuss below.

In the case of rent-stabilization policies, economic theory predicts that overall rent payments should be relatively unaffected. Landlords and tenants should recognize that future rent increases will be limited, and, as a result, landlords should demand more up front from tenants. The implication is higher initial rents for tenants and more modest rent increases over time. Obviously, rent control does limit the ability to front-load payments to the extent that the increases for new tenants are also capped (as in

Newark and Washington). Empirical work has not actually been able to verify or refute this prediction of economic theory.

Economists have emphasized four classes of social loss from rent control which counteract any benefits from the lower rents enjoyed by those who occupy controlled units. Most significantly, lower prices mean less supply. If rent control lowers rents, it will also ensure less building of rental properties and more conversions of the rental stock to owner-occupied condominiums. Olsen (1972) is the classic economic paper showing the supply response to rent control in New York: a decrease in the production of new units and increased conversion to cooperative apartments.

Places like Santa Monica and New York City that exempt new buildings from the harshest rent control are implicitly acknowledging rent control's negative supply effects and trying to reduce them by excluding new buildings from regulation. However, this exclusion will not slow down the conversion of existing rental units to condominiums. Moreover, developers must wonder whether a city that has a well-entrenched rent-control system will be able to resist imposing rent control on new buildings at some future date. There is, then, a real question about whether a policy that claims to exempt new building reasonably can be seen as time consistent.

A second negative effect of rent control is that it limits landlords' incentive to invest in building quality (Frankena 1975). This effect will persist with either rent control or rent stabilization. Rent-control boards have recognized this problem by allowing landlords to petition to increase rents if they have invested in a unit, but given that the rent increases are rarely more than the investment (and may be less), it is hard to see how this provides strong incentives to improve or even maintain quality. With rent stabilization, the landlord has an incentive to improve quality when negotiating with a new tenant, but after that, the landlord loses the incentive.

There is abundant evidence on rent control and quality deterioration. Gyourko and Linneman (1990) document that rent-controlled units in New York City were disproportionately dilapidated. Pollakowski (1999) updates this study and shows a remarkably large number of maintenance problems in rent-controlled apartments. The elimination of rent control in Cambridge was associated with substantial improvement in the quality of the rental stock. Rent-controlled tenants may be paying less for their apartments, but the research shows that they are also getting a lower-quality apartment.

A third cost of rent control arises from the fact that when units rent below market rents, people will exert considerable resources to get those cheap apartments (Barzel 1974; Cheung 1974). According to this view, much of the benefit of cheap apartments gets squandered when prospective tenants expend a great deal of effort and occasionally key money—a cash bribe for the landlord—to get below-market-rent units. This effect is not present in most modern systems where initial rents are determined freely by landlord-tenant negotiations.

A fourth cost associated with rent control is that it leads to a mismatch between renter and apartment (Glaeser and Luttmer 2003). If initial prices are below market rents, then there will be many prospective renters for each apartment, and the allocation will not necessarily be according to willingness to pay. The result of allocating apartments not by willingness to pay but more randomly is that more people who value apartments less will get them. Research has shown that poorer households do not disproportionately receive rent-controlled units (Gyourko and Linneman 1989). Hence, the targeting of program benefits to the poor is weak, too.

Perhaps more relevant for the systems that are in place today, rent stabilization induces people to stay in apartments even as conditions change. Owner-occupiers who no longer use a house fully have the option to sell their home and realize its market value. Renters who are paying below market rents have no natural way of reaping the same benefits. If they want to continue enjoying their below-market rents, they must continue to occupy the unit. A classic example of this is provided in Auletta (1979, 43), which quotes the tobacconist Nat Sherman, whose rent-controlled apartment cost $335 per month: "It happens to be used so little that I think [the rent is] fair." The rent may have captured his valuation of the apartment, but others would have gotten a great deal more value from the unit. It is quite inefficient for an apartment to be occupied by someone who doesn't value it very much.

Overall, it is not possible to make a sound case for rent control. Hard, old-style rent control did reduce rent substantially for covered units, but it also wrought havoc with the broader housing stock. As the Swedish economist Assar Lindbeck (1977, 39) famously said, "next to bombing, rent control seems to be the most efficient technique so far for destroying cities." Moreover, if rent control is meant to redistribute income, then it is hard to see why current landlords are the only people who should pay for that redistribution or why current tenants are its natural recipients. Nobody believes that farmers should be the primary funders of the Food Stamp program. Finally, and most importantly, in the presence of high prices, the obvious goal should be to increase supply, not to decrease it by reducing the incentives for prospective landlords.[2]

Quantity Regulations #1: Building Codes

The regulation of new construction can be separated into the rules regarding land use and the rules regarding building codes. Building codes focus on the materials that can be used in new construction. Land-use regulations focus on what type of buildings can be put on available land. There are some areas where the divisions between the two types of regulations blur, such as rules regarding plumbing (typically considered part of a building code) and those pertaining to septic tanks (typically considered a land-use regulation). Still, it makes sense to distinguish between them, both because they are often administered by different government agents (safety inspectors rather than zoning boards, for example), and because of their different economic impacts.

Building codes generally increase the cost of construction but are unlikely to increase the gap between construction costs and the price of housing. Land-use regulations may also influence construction costs, especially by reducing the scale of new development projects, but in addition they create barriers to building that will directly increase the gap between construction costs and prices. More generally, building codes have a much more limited impact on housing supply than land-use regulations.

Chapter 3's historical review showed that America has never had a completely laissez-faire attitude toward new construction. In the nineteenth century, communities were concerned with building materials because the threat of fire was a real danger for most urban areas. In the Progressive Era, reformers increasingly took aim at overcrowded buildings with limited light and sanitation. In the twentieth century, rules about building materials and unsanitary conditions became even tougher.

Listokin and Hattis (2005) ably summarize the full range of building attributes regulated primarily by local governments. Most places have a series of connected building codes, including a general building code that addresses the basic materials and structure of the building, a plumbing code that deals with water and waste, and an electrical code. Some places also have separate energy codes and have added rules relating to accessibility. Note that at this point, we are addressing those rules that directly pertain to the building structure, not to lot size.

These rules seem to offer benefits to public health and safety, but they also reduce the housing supply because policies that mandate more expensive construction materials or techniques raise building costs and prices. Two literatures have looked at the consequences of restrictions on structure quality for housing affordability. One set of papers asked about the impact of these restrictions on construction costs. The second more specifically focused on whether the destruction of single-room-occupancy (SRO) hotels played a role in increasing homelessness in major cities in the 1980s.

The literature on the relationship between building codes and prices goes back to Maisel (1953), who argued that "building code inefficiencies" increased prices, but that the impact was less than 1 percent. The National Commission on Urban Problems (the Douglas Commission) found that building regulations might be raising prices by as much as 13 percent (Listokin and Hattis 2005). Muth and Wetzler (1976) are closer to Maisel in their estimates and argue that these codes increased prices by less than 2 percent. They pointed to unions as a more significant factor behind high construction costs, a finding more recently reinforced by Gyourko and Saiz (2006). Seidel (1978) and Noam (1983) provide two other estimates of the costs of these restrictions. Seidel actually looked at the differences in the costs of raw material mandated by the codes and estimated a more sizable impact of these regulations. Noam compared more and less restrictive jurisdictions and found an impact on construction costs of around 5 percent.

Our view is that while building codes undoubtedly raise costs, perhaps by as much as 10 percent, they are not the predominant cause of high housing values today. These regulations play a relatively minor role in increasing the costs of housing in America's most expensive jurisdictions, where, as we have already shown, the high cost of housing represents a gap between construction costs and home prices, not high construction costs per se (Glaeser, Gyourko, and Saks 2005).

In the literature looking specifically at building restrictions on single-room-occupancy hotels and their impact on homelessness, time series data show that homelessness rose in the 1980s after a large number of SRO hotels were shut down for failing to meet building codes (O'Flaherty 1996). However, the two primary authors on homelessness give different emphasis to the role of building restrictions in the rise of homelessness. Jencks (1994) emphasizes the deinstitutionalization of mentally troubled individuals. O'Flaherty (1996) sees the regulatory attack on single-room-occupancy hotels as a major reason for the rise of homelessness.

Without taking a stand for either of these authors, we simply note that the rules governing standards for SRO hotels are likely to be more important for a particularly poor segment of the population, but will have little impact on the affordability of housing for most Americans. Still, if O'Flaherty is right, this is yet another cautionary tale about the potential costs of building restrictions. There is no free lunch here: if we eliminate the cheapest housing from the stock, the cost of housing must rise.

Quantity Regulations #2: Land-Use Restrictions

While building codes surely raise costs, their impact seems to be relatively limited. Moreover, it is relatively easy to measure the impact of these codes by directly observing the added costs they impose. Land-use restrictions are quite different, both because there is no natural limit to their impact on price and because assessing their impact is far more difficult conceptually.

Consider the case of an extreme growth-control policy or a new very high minimum-lot-size requirement that completely stopped all new construction within a given locality. Either policy freezes supply at its current level so that there is no ability to respond to any future increases in demand. If the area has an economic collapse, then the growth control is completely irrelevant because no one wants to build there anyway. If the area turns out to be both beautiful and productive, like Silicon Valley, for example, then high demand will ensure extremely high prices because there is no ability of supply to respond. In this case, the price impact of the land-use restriction knows no natural upper bound, but rather will become bigger and bigger as the demand for the area grows.

While the codification of land-use regulations is primarily a twentieth-century phenomenon, even in the nineteenth century communities were passing judgment on what type of development was or was not acceptable. In many areas, developers needed to file for building permits, and even before formal codes were enacted, permits could be denied for structures that were deemed not in the public interest. For example, the hostility of Boston to tall buildings goes back to the nineteenth century, when height limitations were also seen as a means of reducing fire risk.

These pre-building-code restrictions on new construction remind us that land use can be regulated both through formal rules and through informal barriers. For example, a long, drawn-out approval process can occur even if a project seems to meet the formal land-use regulations. Environmental lawsuits have blocked many projects that followed current rules explicitly. In the other direction, it is not unheard of for a new development to receive a waiver that excludes it from existing land-use regulations.

Land-use regulations are remarkably diverse, but the most basic limit the number or size of units that can occupy a given area of land. In lower-density areas, these regulations require minimum lot sizes. In higher-density areas, these regulations limit the height of new buildings. Restrictions on lot sizes and building height go back to the model zoning codes of the early twentieth century. New York City's 1916 zoning code is often described as the first comprehensive ordinance, and it established rules concerning heights and setbacks that were meant to limit the tendency of tall buildings to block out light. While this code has been modified significantly since then, especially in 1961, it remains the pioneer of regulatory attempts to restrict the amount of structure than can be put on a given plot of land.

Rules concerning minimum lot sizes also become widespread after 1916. In the 1920s, communities throughout the United States started to require minimum lot sizes for each new house. This public intervention in planning followed a private-sector tradition in which builders restricted how home buyers in their developments could use land (Fogelson 2007). Today, there is great heterogeneity in the size of the minimum lots allowed by different communities.

Glaeser, Schuetz, and Ward (2006) look at minimum lot sizes across 187 cities and towns in greater Boston (excluding the city of Boston itself). Using Massachusetts Geographical Information Systems (GIS) software, the study calculated the average minimum lot size in each of those jurisdictions. Since minimum lot sizes often differ within jurisdictions, the calculation essen-

FIGURE 4-1

DISTRIBUTION OF SINGLE-FAMILY MINIMUM LOT SIZES,
GREATER BOSTON AREA, 2000

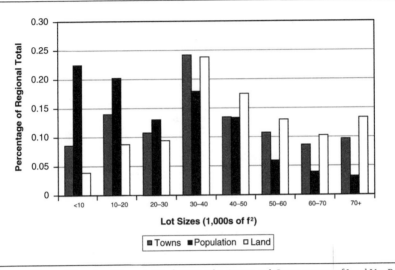

SOURCE: Glaeser, Edward and Bryce A. Ward. 2006. The Causes and Consequences of Land Use Regulation: Evidence from Greater Boston. Working Paper No. W12601, National Bureau of Economic Research. Cambridge, MA.

tially determines averages for those areas where residential construction is allowed.

Figure 4-1 plots the distribution of minimum lot sizes across communities in greater Boston. Within each lot-size category, the fraction of the area's towns, population, and land area is plotted. There is much heterogeneity within this metropolitan area, with some communities having minimum lot sizes of less than one-quarter acre (10,000 ft^2) and other communities having minimum lot sizes of more than two acres. As one might expect, people live disproportionately in those areas with small minimum lot sizes, and land is disproportionately located (relative to people) in areas with large minimum lot sizes.

Since there is such heterogeneity across communities in these minimum lot sizes, it is relatively straightforward to determine whether there is less development in areas with higher minimum lot sizes and whether prices are higher in those areas. Glaeser, Schuetz, and Ward (2006) find that as the average minimum acre per lot in a community rises by one acre, the overall housing stock in the community declines by more than 30 percent. In addition, the level of permitting in the 1990s decreases by more than 30 percent when the study controls for conditions in 1990, and it is estimated to be more than 60 percent lower when the study controls for conditions in 1940.[3] Over the whole 1980–2000 period, an extra acre per lot is associated with around 40 percent less permitting, with 1940 or 1980 controls.[4] More stringent minimum-lot-size regulations (i.e., one-acre versus one-quarter-acre minimums) are associated with substantially less development.

Minimum lot sizes also appear to increase the price of housing. Including 1940-era community controls and housing characteristics, Glaeser, Schuetz, and Ward (2006) find that each acre per lot is associated with a more than 10 percent increase in housing prices. While this price effect does suggest that higher minimum lot sizes make housing less affordable, it is too small to suggest that restricting new construction is "efficient" in that it maximizes the total value of land in the area. Each house costs somewhat more when minimum lot sizes are increased, but there are so many fewer houses that the total value of properties in the community appears to be lower than it would be without the more binding lot-size constraint (Glaeser and Ward 2006).

There is no comparable direct evidence on the impact of restricting building heights. Glaeser, Gyourko, and Saks (2005) do, however, provide indirect evidence that height restrictions on buildings in Manhattan raise condominium prices significantly on that island. Economic theory predicts that in a competitive market for condominiums, the price at which the units sell should equal the cost of supplying them. As noted above, there is every reason to think that the construction industry is inherently competitive, as there are thousands of developers even within New York State. Yet as of 2003, the cost of the average Manhattan condominium was at least double its cost of construction.

The key element in this analysis is that the supply cost of an extra condominium unit in New York City can be calculated by the cost of building up. An extra floor on a high-rise building requires no extra land acquisition. As such, the cost of supplying extra space should be just the construction cost of the next story. Glaeser, Gyourko, and Saks (2005) show that the cost of adding an extra floor for the typical building is about $300 per square foot during the study's sample period, but that condominiums were selling for at least double that amount on average.

In the absence of height restrictions, this price differential creates a profound incentive to build taller buildings. However, new apartment buildings have not been getting taller in Manhattan over the past thirty years. New apartment buildings have been getting shorter. While more than 80 percent of new units in Manhattan in the 1970s were in buildings of more than twenty stories, less than 40 percent of new units supplied in the 1990s were in buildings of more than twenty stories (Glaeser, Gyourko, and Saks 2005). Over this same time period, prices soared. Only binding height restrictions can explain how builders erected shorter and shorter buildings as New York City real estate became more and more valuable.

While minimum lot sizes and height restrictions may be the most straightforward of all land-use restrictions, there are many others. Growth controls, which were adopted in many California communities in the 1970s, also work to reduce supply. These restrictions limit the extent of new building in a year in a community. Katz and Rosen (1987) compare communities in Northern California and finds that growth controls are associated with substantially more expensive housing.

Today, communities have enacted rules concerning wetlands, septic systems, and subdivisions, all of which can make it more difficult to build. Figure 4-2 shows the rise over time in the number of communities in greater Boston that have adopted such rules. In addition, communities have enacted increasingly stringent rules over time. While these rules may have legitimate public purposes, they are often worded in an extremely vague fashion. In addition, rules can be strikingly different across similar communities. If land-use regulations were responding to a common need to protect wetlands and treat waste, then similar places should have similar codes. Yet the codes differ enormously, which suggests regulatory randomness more than environmental need.

Glaeser and Ward (2006) look at the impact of these rules on permitting and prices. Comparing communities before and after these rules were established, this study finds that permitting declines by about 10 percent after a new type of rule is enacted. It also finds a significantly positive price impact of enacting these rules.

FIGURE 4-2

FRACTION OF COMMUNITIES IN GREATER BOSTON WITH WETLANDS,
SEPTIC, SUBDIVISION, AND CLUSTER PROVISIONS, 1975–2004

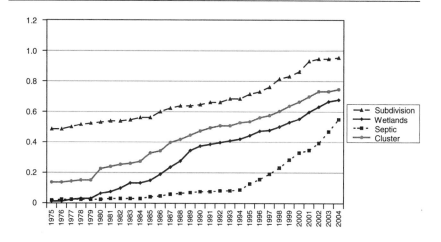

SOURCE: Glaeser, Edward and Bryce A. Ward. 2006. The Causes and Consequences of Land Use Regulation: Evidence from Greater Boston. Working Paper No. W12601, National Bureau of Economic Research. Cambridge, MA.
NOTE: Communities that adopt provisions at unknown dates are excluded from fraction.

Given the vagueness of many of these regulations and the differences in implementation, it is useful to look at more general measures of how stringently different areas control new construction. These measures are found in Gyourko, Saiz, and Summers (2008a), which reports on the Wharton Residential Land Use Regulatory Index. The authors surveyed over 2,600 jurisdictions, asking a battery of questions about the overall residential land-use regulatory environment. These questions deal mainly with outcomes, such as approval times, and with the involvement of different political actors in the approval process. The research uses principal component analysis to produce a single index that measures the overall degree of barriers to development across each of these different communities. The survey was conducted mostly in 2005, so it should reflect fairly recent conditions.[5]

The index number increases with the difficulty of new construction, so that the more positive the index, the more intensely regulated the community. Lower index values indicate less-regulated places. The index also is normalized to have a mean of zero and a standard deviation of one. This is a standard normalization which signifies that the value of the index does not have any meaning in an absolute sense, but rather tells how many other communities are less regulated than the community in question.

Using this index, Gyourko, Saiz, and Summers (2008a) look at well over 160 jurisdictions nationwide with index values very close to zero in order to gauge what it means to have the "average" regulatory climate pertaining to local land-use controls. The typical local land-use regulatory climate for a community within one of the nation's metropolitan areas is as follows: (a) two entities are required to approve any project that requires a zoning change; one of these entities typically is a zoning commission, while the other is a group such as the city council or an environmental review board; requiring multiple approvals makes it easier to stop any project, and the data show this is now the norm in the United States; (b) some type of minimum-lot-size constraint is in place, although it is unlikely to be as onerous as a one-half- or one-acre minimum; thus, lot-size regulations to control density are now virtually omnipresent in communities across the United States; (c) exactions and open-space requirements also tend to exist in these average places, although there are some typical communities without open-space requirements; and (d) there is about a six-month lag on average between the submission of a permit application and permit issuance on a standard project for the community; this is far less than what is standard for highly regulated communities, where a long lag is one of the key ways in which new residential development is delayed or stopped.

While the typical place is far from unregulated, the intensity of local land-use controls varies widely by geography. Table 4-1's presentation of the average index values for communities in each of the four census regions and their nine associated divisions shows that communities in states on the two coasts tend to be much more highly regulated than others. For example, the average index value for all 640 communities in the East census region is 0.65, indicating that these places have regulatory climates that are about two-thirds of a standard deviation above the norm for the country. This value means that approximately two-thirds of all places have regulatory environments that are more liberal than the average place in this region.

The towns in the six states in the New England census division are the most highly regulated in the country, averaging almost a full standard

TABLE 4-1

WHARTON RESIDENTIAL LAND USE REGULATORY INDEX (WRLURI),
BY CENSUS REGION AND DIVISION

	Average index value	Number of communities
East region	0.65	640
Northestern division	0.98	261
Mid-Atlantic division	0.42	379
Midwest region	−0.39	818
East North Central division	−0.22	525
West North Central division	−0.70	293
South region	−0.38	690
South Atlantic division	−0.08	320
East South Central divison	−0.75	127
West South Central division	−0.57	243
West region	0.35	465
Pacific division	0.51	281
Mountain division	0.11	184

SOURCE: Gyourko, Joseph E., Albert Saiz, and Anita A. Summers. 2008a. A new measure of the local regulatory environment for housing markets: Wharton Residential Land Use Regulatory Index. *Urban Studies* 45, no. 3: 693–729.
NOTES: Index values are from the Wharton Residential Land Use Regulation Project (Gyourko, Saiz, and Summers 2008a). An index value of 0 implies the average level of regulation in the country. An index value of 1 implies a level of regulation one standard deviation above the national average. An index value of -1 implies a level of regulation one standard deviation below the national average.

deviation above the national average. This implies that more than 80 percent of all places are less regulated than these areas. Places in the Midwest and South regions are the most lightly regulated in America, as indicated by their negative index values. Finally, the West census region tends to be more highly regulated than the national average, but there is great heterogeneity across states in that part of the country.

Tables 4-2 and 4-3 reproduce results from Gyourko, Saiz, and Summers (2008a) showing index values for all fifty states and for forty-seven metropolitan areas where more than ten communities responded to the survey.

TABLE 4-2

WHARTON RESIDENTIAL LAND USE REGULATORY INDEX (WRLURI),
BY STATE

State	WRLURI	Number of observations
1. Hawaii	2.34	1
2. Rhode Island	1.56	17
3. Massachusetts	1.52	79
4. New Hampshire	1.37	32
5. New Jersey	0.89	104
6. Maryland	0.81	18
7. Washington	0.71	49
8. Maine	0.64	44
9. California	0.62	182
10. Arizona	0.60	40
11. Colorado	0.51	48
12. Delaware	0.51	5
13. Florida	0.38	97
14. Pennsylvania	0.36	182
15. Connecticut	0.35	65
16. Vermont	0.33	24
17. Minnesota	0.10	80
18. Oregon	0.09	42
19. Wisconsin	0.09	93
20. Michigan	0.03	111
21. Utah	–0.05	41
22. New Mexico	–0.08	16
23. New York	–0.12	92
24. Illinois	–0.17	139
25. Virginia	–0.20	35
26. Georgia	–0.20	56
27. North Carolina	–0.33	64
28. Montana	–0.33	6
29. Ohio	–0.37	135
30. Wyoming	–0.43	7
31. Texas	–0.45	165

continued on next page

Table 4-2 continued

State	WRLURI	Number of observations
32. Nevada	–0.45	7
33. North Dakota	–0.55	8
34. Kentucky	–0.58	28
35. Idaho	–0.62	19
36. Tennessee	–0.67	41
37. Nebraska	–0.67	22
38. Oklahoma	–0.70	36
39. South Carolina	–0.75	30
40. Mississippi	–0.83	21
41. Arkansas	–0.87	23
42. West Virginia	–0.93	15
43. Alabama	–0.94	37
44. Iowa	–0.99	59
45. South Dakota	–1.01	11
46. Alaska	–1.01	7
47. Indiana	–1.02	47
48. Missouri	–1.02	67
49. Louisiana	–1.07	19
50. Kansas	–1.11	46

Source: Gyourko, Saiz, and Summers 2008a, table 10.
Note: An index value of 0 signifies the average degree of regulation in the country.

These data confirm that there is a strong positive correlation between being on the coast and having a highly regulated residential land-use regime. In addition, the metropolitan area table confirms that markets in the Northeast are the most highly regulated in the nation, with Providence, Boston, and Monmouth-Ocean (suburban New Jersey) topping the table. Denver is the only interior market listed in the top ten. Phoenix's number eleven ranking is interesting and suggests that the Sunbelt market has increased the strictness of its local land-use controls in recent years.

Across metropolitan areas, this index is strongly related to prices. Figure 4-3 documents the strong positive correlation between the average price in a metropolitan area and the index average across the jurisdictions

TABLE 4-3

WHARTON RESIDENTIAL LAND USE REGULATORY INDEX (WRLURI),
BY METROPOLITAN AREAS WITH TEN OR MORE OBSERVATIONS

Metropolitan area	WRLURI	Number of observations
1. Providence-Fall River-Warwick, RI-MA	1.79	16
2. Boston, MA-NH	1.54	41
3. Monmouth-Ocean, NJ	1.21	15
4. Philadelphia, PA	1.03	55
5. Seattle-Bellevue-Everett, WA	1.01	21
6. San Francisco, CA	0.90	13
7. Denver, CO	0.85	13
8. Nassau-Suffolk, NY	0.80	14
9. Bergen-Passaic, NJ	0.71	21
10. Fort Lauderdale, FL	0.70	16
11. Phoenix-Mesa, AZ	0.70	18
12. New York, NY	0.63	19
13. Riverside-San Bernardino, CA	0.61	20
14. Newark, NJ	0.60	25
15. Springfield, MA	0.58	13
16. Harrisburg-Lebanon-Carlise, PA	0.55	15
17. Oakland, CA	0.52	12
18. Los Angeles-Long Beach, CA	0.51	32
19. Hartford, CT	0.50	28
20. San Diego, CA	0.48	11
21. Orange County, CA	0.39	14
22. Minneapolis-St. Paul, MN-WI	0.34	48
23. Washington, DC-MD-VA-WV	0.33	12
24. Portland-Vancouver, OR-WA	0.29	20
25. Milwaukee-Waukesha, WI	0.25	21
26. Akron, OH	0.15	11
27. Detroit, MI	0.12	46
28. Allentown-Bethlehem-Easton, PA	0.10	14
29. Chicago, IL	0.06	95
30. Pittsburgh, PA	0.06	44
31. Atlanta, GA	0.04	26

continued on next page

Table 4-3 continued

Metropolitan area	WRLURI	Number of observations
32. Scranton-Wilkes-Barre-Hazelton, PA	0.03	11
33. Salt Lake City-Ogden, UT	−0.10	19
34. Grand Rapids-Muskegon-Holland, MI	−0.15	16
35. Cleveland-Lorain-Elyria, OH	−0.16	31
36. Rochester, NY	−0.17	12
37. Tampa-St. Petersburg-Clearwater, FL	−0.17	12
38. San Antonio, TX	−0.24	12
39. Fort Worth-Arlington, TX	−0.27	15
40. Houston, TX	−0.33	14
41. Dallas, TX	−0.35	31
42. Oklahoma City, OK	−0.41	12
43. Dayton-Springfield, OH	−0.50	17
44. Cincinnati, OH-KY-IN	−0.56	27
45. St. Louis, MO-IL	−0.72	27
46. Indianapolis, IN	−0.76	12
47. Kansas City, MO-KS	−0.80	29

SOURCE: Gyourko, Saiz, and Summers 2008a, table 10.
NOTE: An index value of 0 signifies the average degree of regulation in the country.

that were surveyed in the sample. This figure includes only the forty-three metropolitan areas with more than ten jurisdictions responding to the Wharton survey that could be matched with metropolitan area house price data.[6] The overall correlation between the index and prices is 60 percent. A one standard deviation increase in the index is associated with about a $133,000 increase in house prices, an amount that roughly approximates the physical construction costs of an average quality home.

A higher regulatory index value also is correlated with less permitting, but this relationship is clouded by the fact that markets in very low demand also should have very low permitting rates. Figure 4-4 graphs the relationship between the Wharton index and the amount of permitting for the thirty-eight metropolitan areas that had average house values above $110,000. Permitting is measured by the ratio of all permits issued between 2000 and 2006 to the size of the housing stock in the year 2000. There is

FIGURE 4-3

HOME PRICES AND LOCAL LAND-USE REGULATION

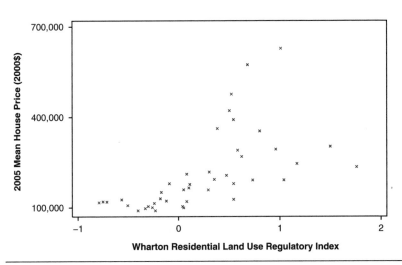

SOURCES: Office of Federal Housing Enterprise Oversight. Repeat Sales House Price Index. Washington, D.C.: Office of Federal Housing Enterprise Oversight, 1993–2008; U.S. Census Bureau. 2000 Decennial Census, County Housing Characteristics. Washington, D.C.: U.S. Census Bureau, 2000; Gyourko, Saiz, and Summers. 2008. Wharton Residential Land Use Regulation Index. http://real.wharton.upenn.edu/~gyourko/Wharton_residential_land_use_reg.html.

a statistically significant negative relationship between the two series, with the overall correlation being –0.38.[7] The simple regression of the permit share variable on the Wharton index implies that a one standard deviation increase in the index is associated with a 4.4 point decline in the permit share. Once again, one cannot impute causality from such a simple exercise, but the raw data are consistent with more regulation lowering the amount of homebuilding activity in the market

We already know from figure 2-11 that areas that build a great deal are not expensive, and areas that are expensive do not build a great deal. As we have already argued, the difference between San Francisco and Las Vegas in that graph cannot be driven by differences in demand. If demand was the only thing that differed across metropolitan areas, then we would expect to see some areas with high prices and much construction and some with low prices and little construction. Instead, we see that places with high prices

FIGURE 4-4

PERMITS AND LOCAL LAND-USE REGULATION

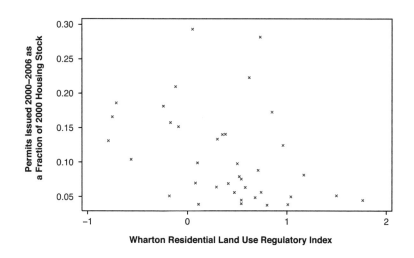

SOURCES: Gyourko, Saiz, and Summers. 2008. Wharton Residential Land Use Regulation Index. http://real.wharton.upenn.edu/~gyourko/Wharton_residential_land_use_reg.html; U.S. Census Bureau Manufacturing, Mining and Construction Statistics. County Building Permits 2000–2004. Washington, D.C.: U.S. Census Bureau, 2000–2004; U.S. Census Bureau. 2000 Decennial Census, County Housing Characteristics. Washington, D.C.: U.S. Census Bureau, 2000.

have little construction and places with much construction have low prices. Only differences in supply can explain this heterogeneity.

Measures of community wealth, but not population density, are strongly positively correlated with the intensity of local land-use regulation in the Gyourko, Saiz, and Summers (2008a) survey data. Those data show that the greater the median family income, median house value, or share of adults with college degrees in the community, the higher the community's regulatory index value. If highly regulated communities are expensive because these places literally are running out of land, then we would expect a strongly positive correlation between density and index values. However, the correlation between population density and the regulatory index is modestly negative, which reflects the fact that a number of very low-density towns have some of the most tightly regulated local land-use environments in the country. This fact supports the view that fundamental land scarcity is not the primary motivation for strict land-use controls. While correlation cannot be construed as causality from these data, the strong positive relation of regulatory strictness with various measures of community wealth suggests exclusionary desires are a key factor in many places.

One further aspect of land-use control we have not addressed thus far is the impact fee that charges developers for costs allegedly associated with new construction. In some states, like California and Florida, impact fees have become quite common. In other states, like Massachusetts, they are not legally permitted. Adding an impact fee to an existing set of regulatory rules creates yet another cost for developers, which will surely reduce the supply of housing and raise its price, all else constant. But if these fees substitute for other rules, they can be an improvement. Unlike a multiyear approval process that is full of uncertainty and that generates costs for development with no offsetting benefits, a clear impact-fee policy potentially offers the benefits of clarity, speed, and revenues.[8]

Recent research also indicates that house prices are more volatile, not just higher, in tightly regulated markets. In their examination of house prices and new construction during the two large national price swings of the past quarter century, Glaeser, Gyourko, and Saiz (2008) document that during both the boom of the late 1980s and the more recent one beginning in the mid-1990s, price increases were much higher in markets that were more supply constrained. During the housing bust of the early 1990s, prices also fell more in these markets.

That research also shows that price bubbles are more likely to form in tightly regulated places, because the inelastic supply conditions that are created in part from strict local land-use regulation are an important factor in supporting ever larger price increases whenever demand is increasing. It is more difficult for house prices to become too disconnected from their fundamental production costs in lightly regulated markets because significant new supply quickly dampens prices, thereby busting any illusions market participants might have about the potential for ever larger price increases.

In the freer, more unregulated markets, permitting intensity was very high during the boom of the early to mid-1980s, and prices remained close to their fundamental production costs. The more recent boom saw a few such markets (e.g., Orlando and Phoenix) experience temporary price explosions, but the length of these pricing booms still is much shorter than those in the more tightly regulated, supply-constrained coastal markets. Even with the abnormally high price appreciation in some elastically supplied markets, price growth still was much higher during the recent boom. Between 1996 and 2006, average real house price appreciation was a whopping 47 percentage points greater in the more supply-constrained markets. Real prices escalated by 81 percent in the more constrained markets versus 34 percent in the less constrained ones.[9] Thus, the recent boom was widespread, but it still was much larger in the more highly regulated coastal markets, and middle-class affordability conditions deteriorated the most in those places. This indicates that housing supply conditions, not just mortgage markets, play an important role in accounting for the nature of booms and busts in different areas.

Thus, basic economics and the data are consistent with local land-use regulations having a dramatic impact on U.S. housing markets. Places with high housing demand and abundant land-use restrictions have limited supply and high prices. Places that have met high housing demand with much less restriction on development have become the fastest growing regions of the country. Since 2000, the four metropolitan areas with the greatest population growth in the country are Atlanta, Dallas, Houston, and Riverside-San Bernardino. These areas have added more homes than New York or Los Angeles or Chicago. Their growth does not reflect extraordinary economic vitality or delightful Mediterranean climates. Instead, homes are being built in those places because their communities are much more pro-development than communities in coastal California. The fact that local land-use decisions are having such an impact on the shape of America presents another reason why the federal government should have policies that address these decisions.

While local land-use decisions do have a major impact on U.S. housing prices, eliminating those restrictions entirely still would not result in uniform prices across the country. Demand would still be higher in some places than others. Construction costs would also vary, and as land became scarcer in denser areas, prices would rise in those places. Yet the differences in prices would still be far less stark. Moreover, in an unregulated world, these differences would clearly reflect the workings of the market, not the decisions of local zoning boards.

Of course, even if we accept that land-use regulations restrict development and increase prices, it does not follow that local zoning boards always make bad decisions. Perhaps new development should be restricted in some areas because of the environmental and aesthetic externalities that are associated with new homes. On theoretical grounds, at least, land-use regulations might decrease affordability while still being quite rational and efficient.

There are four strong reasons why this is probably not so in actuality. First, the sheer randomness of rules across jurisdictions is hard to reconcile with the view that these rules are rationally responding to local environmental (or other) needs. Institutional differences such as county-level control over land use in Maryland versus town-level control in Massachusetts seem to be quite important in driving permitting. In general, larger jurisdictions that contain businesses as well as homes are more permissive, probably because business owners want their workers to be able to afford homes in the area. These institutional factors don't seem to reflect differences in the real externalities associated with development.

Second, as we have already argued, even when local land-use decisions are motivated by seemingly sound environmental arguments, they rarely take into account the global environmental consequences of restricting new supply. For example, environmentalists on the San Francisco Bay may be able to block a higher-density project in their backyards, which seems to help the local environment. However, restrictive local regulation does not stop development in the United States. That development just moves someplace else, and building in the desert outside of Las Vegas well may be worse for the environment than building near Oakland. In general, local land-use policy pushes building from areas where there are people to areas where there are fewer neighbors to object. It is hard for us to imagine that moving development into the lowest-density areas is good environmentalism, and we know it is not good land-use planning.

Third, good decision making is likely to occur only if property rights are well defined, so that costs to neighbors if construction goes forward are weighed against costs to the property owner if construction is blocked. However, few areas have a clear mechanism that would push local decision makers to weigh these costs and benefits well. Instead, democratic governance tends to give sway to the more numerous neighbors over a single property owner, even if that owner suffers hugely from being denied the right to build and each neighbor suffers only a minute loss.

Fourth, the available empirical evidence suggests that land-use restrictions are certainly not maximizing total land value in a community, which is a standard condition for efficient land-use policies. According to a long-standing result in urban economics, optimal development occurs when the land value in a community is maximized. That is, efficiently weighing the benefits to builders and the costs to neighbors means that new development proceeds whenever the benefits exceed the costs. The finding by Glaeser, Schuetz, and Ward (2006) that total land values would increase with more density in much of suburban Boston—that is, that land value is not maximized under current policy—strongly suggests that land-use regulations are not efficient but rather excessively restrictive.

Hybrid Price and Quantity Controls: Inclusionary Zoning

We have so far discussed regulations that purely target price (rent control) and regulations that purely target quantity (land-use restrictions). In recent years, there has been increasing interest in a hybrid approach that combines price and quantity regulations. Inclusionary zoning is the most common policy that melds controls on price and controls on quantity.

This type of policy is best understood as an attempt to leverage localities' ability to control new development into an ability to control prices as well. As we have already discussed, most states have stopped their localities from imposing explicit rent controls, but local jurisdictions still have a fairly unfettered ability to control new development. By linking new development to the provision of affordable units, localities are managing to provide below-market-rate housing that they could not typically generate with a rent-control ordinance because of state legislative restrictions.

Inclusionary zoning requires that a share of homes in any new development (typically between 10 and 30 percent) be "affordable." Affordability is generally defined by sales price in the case of owner-occupied housing and rent in the case of rental units. In most cases, there also is an income ceiling on who may be allowed to buy or rent these units. Typically, the residents of affordable units must earn less than some multiple of the median income or poverty-level income in the region. In many cases, the limit on the sales price persists after the initial sale, implying that subsequent owners also pay less than the market price for the unit.

These rules are fairly new, and they have not been uniformly implemented in different areas. For both of these reasons, statistical work on these policies is difficult, and there has been very little empirical study of the impact of inclusionary zoning. Hence, we must fall back on an economic analysis of these rules. On one level, these rules certainly do ensure that more housing deemed affordable is built. By their nature, they provide a few clearly observable units that fit some desirable price threshold. The highly measurable aspect of these produced units is one of the reasons why these policies have been so attractive to many jurisdictions.

However, the actual count of new "affordable" units produced tells us little about the overall impact of these policies on housing affordability. Requiring developers to produce affordable units is essentially a tax on market-rate development that should reduce the overall level of building. In general, there will be a number of highly observable affordable units, but there will also be a less visible loss of new units which will make housing less affordable.[10]

If the goal is to reduce the equilibrium price of housing, then it is the overall number of units being produced that matters. A new "tax" on development created by inclusionary zoning rules will reduce that number of units and make housing for the average buyer less affordable. These rules well may end up being counterproductive by making housing less profitable to build.

The one caveat to this analysis is that it is impossible to tell what the regulatory environment would have been in the absence of these rules. If inclusionary zoning is a new requirement on building that simply increases the barriers to new construction, then it will surely reduce the amount of building. However, if inclusionary zoning makes it possible for builders to avoid other barriers, or if these rules substitute for others that would have been put in place, then the impact of inclusionary zoning is more benign. For example, if inclusionary zoning is essentially a means for developers to pay some cost that allows them to avoid other existing rules, then it could increase supply and make housing more affordable.

Massachusetts Chapter 40B. One of the older forms of inclusionary zoning in the country is Massachusetts's Comprehensive Permit Law, typically referred to as Massachusetts Chapter 40B. This law is a hybrid regulation that combines price and quantity rules. Enacted in 1969, it has many provisions, most of which have little to do with inclusionary zoning or affordable housing. However, it has become known primarily for a provision (40B) designed to make affordable housing easier to build.

Recognizing the difficulties that local zoning boards often created for building affordable units, Chapter 40B established an alternative zoning process available to developments that meet at least two major criteria. First, the developments must be in cities or towns where less than 10 percent of the housing is affordable according to the program's definition. Second, more than one-fifth of the units in the development must be priced (or rented) below market and must go to lower-income individuals. Chapter 40B is not available to every developer but can be used only by public agencies, nonprofits, and private developers with federal assistance to build low-income housing. A variety of other less important rules must also be met by the development.

If a town has sufficiently little affordable housing, then a developer promising to build enough affordable units could essentially sidestep local zoning boards and build according to a more lenient set of state-mandated rules. A 40B project still goes through a local zoning process, but if the local zoning board rejects the project, the decision can be overruled by the more lenient Zoning Board of Appeals.

There are no centrally collected estimates on the number of units directly built under Chapter 40B. One estimate is that twenty-one thousand units were built between 1970 and 1999 (Krefetz n.d.). Other estimates are that up to forty-three thousand units were constructed through 2006 and that 30 percent of all housing built in Massachusetts between 2003 and 2006 was built using Chapter 40B directly (Citizens' Housing and Planning Association 2006). While the program does seem to be associated with considerable construction, it is also quite unpopular, and in some cities and towns affordable housing was built over local opposition.

In fact, it is hard to know just how much housing is really associated with Chapter 40B, because developers can use it as a threat to get communities to approve non-40B projects. Certainly there are allegations that developers have pressured communities to accept normal, non-40B projects by threatening to build affordable units under 40B if the normal projects are rejected. Indeed, as long as neither the town nor the developer really wants affordable units, each party has strong incentives to come to a bargain that avoids those units. The power of Chapter 40B as a threat, however, is limited by the fact that it can be used only by those developers with access to government subsidies.

A comparison of Chapter 40B and standard inclusionary zoning rules makes it clear that these hybrid regulations can either increase or decrease housing supply, meaning that the details really matter for this type of regulation. Chapter 40B unambiguously strengthens housing supply in Massachusetts because it gives developers more options and more bargaining power. It does not impose new requirements, but gives builders an escape hatch to avoid local zoning boards. This situation makes clear that in judging a policy's impact on housing supply and overall housing affordability, we should look at whether it imposes additional costs on development or provides developers more options, not on specific rules about affordable housing units.

The Mount Laurel Decision. Another long-standing housing market intervention that combines price and quantity regulation is the Mount Laurel ruling, a dramatic challenge to local zoning power that came from the New Jersey Supreme Court. In the early 1970s, a New Jersey nonprofit, the Springville Action Council, tried to build affordable housing with state subsidy in Mount Laurel, New Jersey. These units were meant to house Mount Laurel residents who had been evicted through the township's efforts at urban renewal. Mount Laurel repeatedly refused to permit the project.

The NAACP then joined the Springville Action Council and initiated a lawsuit that ultimately went to the state supreme court. The court ruled against the township, but the principle for which this case became famous did not become clear until eight years later, when the New Jersey Supreme Court spoke again in *Mount Laurel II*, which required towns not only to allow but to provide incentives for affordable housing. Specifically, it declared that land-use "regulations that do not provide the requisite opportunity for a 'fair share' of the region's need for low- and moderate-income housing conflict with the general welfare and violate the state constitutional requirements of substantive due process and equal protection."[11] This ruling also established new judicial positions that would directly oversee the implementation of the program.

Eventually the Mount Laurel ruling came to resemble Massachusetts 40B, in that it allowed developments that included affordable units to bypass the local land-use controls imposed by communities with few of those units. The Mount Laurel ruling was, if anything, far more sweeping, since there were fewer restrictions on the developers who could apply for relief and more communities that were affected by it.

The final twist, though, came from the state legislature. In 1985, the Fair Housing Act was passed, which introduced Regional Contribution Agreements (RCAs) into the equation. These agreements made it possible for a town to satisfy its obligation to build affordable housing by paying for that housing to be constructed somewhere else within the same region of New Jersey. Essentially, wealthy suburbs were able to pay poor cities to take affordable housing out of their own backyard and build it elsewhere. To date, more than $200 million has been transferred through the system, and more than ten thousand units of housing have been built. RCAs are overseen by a new Council of Affordable Housing, which took over much of the administration of the Mount Laurel System.

The RCA system is certainly imperfect, but it has some attractive features. Communities that are willing to pay a lot to avoid affordable housing can give money to poorer communities that don't mind as much. The system in general seems to redistribute from rich to poor, and it does produce more housing. As we will discuss later, the system could perhaps be improved by recognizing that all housing is not the same. It is, in a sense, a starting point for a policy that both respects local control over land use and pushes against the tendency of localities to overly restrict new development.

While inclusionary zoning schemes can be beneficial, those benefits should not be overstated. We believe that some new development has occurred because of programs such as Massachusetts's 40B and New Jersey's RCA program, but neither Massachusetts nor New Jersey has become a bastion of affordable housing, for the middle class or the poor. (We should look to Texas, not Massachusetts or New Jersey, for guidance in making low-cost homes available to ordinary Americans.) In general, inclusionary zoning programs represent a tax on new market-rate development, so some market units that would have been delivered in the absence of the tax are not delivered. Hence, the net contribution of these programs in terms of new housing supply is less than the number of "affordable" units delivered. In sum, one cannot expect a policy that effectively taxes developers to produce enough new housing to solve any significant affordability problem.

Conclusion

Maximum rent ceilings, a classic price control, used to be the most prominent housing market regulation. But the destructive consequences of this policy for the broader housing market are now well understood. Most importantly, this policy weakens incentives for new supply, so it cannot help to solve an affordability crisis in which prices are well above production costs. Rent control is also an incredibly inefficient way to redistribute resources to the poor for housing consumption. Fortunately, rent controls presently exist in cities in only four states, and the new control regimes tend to be milder than the WWII-era schemes. We do not anticipate a widespread return to this policy, although a recent proposal in Boston to enact collective rent bargaining could be more pernicious in its consequences than even New York City's old-style control regime.

Quality and quantity restrictions have replaced price controls in the arsenal of housing regulation. Building codes have become more burdensome, and the data indicate that they could account for up to a 10 percent increase in house prices. But a 10 percent price increase does not explain the bulk of the very large increases in house prices observed in many U.S. markets. The expansion of land-use controls and regulations is a much greater influence in causing housing prices to rise. This type of regulation has proliferated in scale and complexity, and analyses of the Boston area and the new Wharton index strongly suggest that quantity and quality controls significantly contribute to high house prices in markets where those values are well above construction costs.

We see local land-use restrictions as something of a government-created market failure. In principle, these rules could efficiently internalize the social costs of development (e.g., pollution, crowding), but there is very little reason to think that they actually do so. Instead, it seems that heterogeneity in these policies across space reflects local politics more than anything else; and at least in some areas, the restrictions seem far too onerous relative to what is needed to compensate residents for the added social costs of new development. These local rules have had a massive impact on the affordability of American housing. If we are to make housing more affordable, then checking these local rules seems like the first order of business.

Inclusionary zoning schemes have been implemented in some markets in hopes of generating more "affordable" housing, where "affordable" implies valuations below those presently existing in the market. If properly designed, these schemes can generate some additional housing, but they will not solve the underlying affordability problem in high-cost housing markets. The reason is that they essentially tax market-rate development, which fundamentally limits the supply-generating capacity of the program.

5

Other Interventions in Housing Markets—Taxes and Subsidies

While the direct controls on price and new building that we just looked at have an impressive and often adverse impact on housing markets, indirect interventions have a much more obvious impact on the federal government's bottom line. The tax treatment of home mortgages alone involves at least $75 billion worth of extra deductions. Voucher programs and the Low Income Housing Tax Credit also cost many billions of dollars. The key question, of course, is whether their benefits exceed their costs.

In this chapter, we analyze four major subsidy programs related to the housing market and look at their impacts on housing affordability. We deal first with the largest program, the subsidy to homeowners through the tax code. We also look at various implicit subsidies to the housing-related government-sponsored enterprises; at the Low Income Housing Tax Credit program, which provides subsidies to developers for the construction of affordable housing; and at tenant-based subsidies offered via Section 8 vouchers for the consumption of affordable housing.

The Tax Code and Homeownership

To non-economists, the federal tax policy toward homeownership is distinguished mainly by the fact that interest payments and local property taxes are deductible. Economists flip this around and ask instead why the benefits that accrue from investing in a home are not taxed. A classic definition of a tax shelter investment is one in which expenses can be deducted without having to declare any income. Owner-occupied housing remains one of the few such tax shelters available under U.S. tax law. Homeowners may deduct mortgage interest and local property taxes without having to report any imputed rental income on the home.[1]

The home mortgage interest deduction is something of a political sacred cow, but that does not make it good policy. The policy reduces the tax burden for homeowners in a way that strongly favors wealthier Americans (Poterba and Sinai 2008). Are the benefits of this deduction enough to justify a significant decrease in tax revenues that favors the richest taxpayers?

It is generally accepted both that the favorable tax benefits of homeownership in the United States stimulate the demand for housing,[2] and that this subsidy comes at a significant fiscal cost in terms of tax expenditures. Carasso, Steuerle, and Bell (2005) show that federal housing tax expenditures in fiscal year 2005 were well over three times greater than direct spending on housing programs ($147 billion in tax expenditures versus $41 billion in actual outlays).[3]

The subsidy to owners also is very large. Sinai and Gyourko (2004, 188, table 1) report an aggregate gross subsidy of $420 billion in 2000, with the typical owner receiving $6,024 in benefits that year.[4] This is an economically large number, as its discounted long-term value, assuming a 7 percent rate, is $86,057 (i.e., $6,024/.07 = $86,057). However, this does not mean that housing is cheaper by this amount for the typical owner. One reason is that the program is not free and must be paid for in some way. Precisely how it is paid for within the complexity of the U.S. tax and fiscal system is not clear, but owners still can benefit if part of the costs are paid by renters.

The home mortgage interest deduction effectively redistributes from taxpayers with low taxes, low incomes, and low house values to those with high taxes, high incomes, and high house values; this is so because the subsidy is greater as house prices, debt levels, and marginal tax rates rise. Sinai and Gyourko (2004) show that these factors interact with one another to produce very large subsidy flows to owners concentrated in the major metropolitan areas along the east and west coasts of the nation. Thus, there is systematic variation across states and metropolitan areas in the determinants of subsidy values, even though the federal tax code obviously is national in scope.

The extent of the variation in benefits across space is illustrated by the data reported in table 5-1, which reproduces the aggregate subsidy flow estimates by state from Sinai and Gyourko (2004) for the year 1999 (which

TABLE 5-1
AGGREGATE BENEFIT FLOW IN BILLIONS OF 1999$

State	Aggregate benefit flow
Alabama	4.18
Alaska	0.67
Arizona	6.55
Arkansas	2.09
California	78.66
Colorado	8.56
Connecticut	8.23
Delaware	1.20
District of Columbia	1.41
Florida	19.62
Georgia	10.49
Hawaii	2.91
Idaho	1.55
Illinois	19.71
Indiana	6.13
Iowa	3.07
Kansas	2.93
Kentucky	3.81
Louisiana	3.49
Maine	1.59
Maryland	9.56
Massachusetts	14.03
Michigan	17.59
Minnesota	7.67
Mississippi	2.00
Missouri	6.11
Montana	1.04
Nebraska	1.67
Nevada	2.30
New Hampshire	1.74
New Jersey	17.60
New Mexico	2.15
New York	39.72

continued on next page

Table 5-1 continued

State	Aggregate benefit flow
North Carolina	10.54
North Dakota	0.41
Ohio	13.32
Oklahoma	2.67
Oregon	6.48
Pennsylvania	13.82
Rhode Island	1.49
South Carolina	4.76
South Dakota	0.48
Tennesseee	5.61
Texas	15.60
Utah	3.21
Vermont	0.72
Virginia	10.90
Washington	9.52
West Virginia	1.40
Wisconsin	8.64
Wyoming	0.46

SOURCE: Sinai and Gyourko 2004.

is based on data from the 2000 census). Not surprisingly, the most populous state, California, reaps the greatest benefit, with almost $79 billion in
program benefits flowing to its homeowners. No other state approaches
that level of subsidy; New York, whose owners receive over $39 billion, is
second. Even on a per-owner basis, people in a small number of states
receive substantially more tax-code-related benefits than does the typical
owner nationally. California no longer is the extreme outlier it is in the
aggregate data, but it is one of only seven states that received more than
$8,000 per owner in 1999.

The spatial distribution of benefits is even more skewed at the metropolitan area level. The left panel of table 5-2 uses data from Sinai and
Gyourko (2004) on the benefits per owner-occupied unit for the twenty
metropolitan areas with the highest subsidy amounts per owner; the right
panel provides the analogous information for the twenty areas with the

TABLE 5-2

BENEFITS PER OWNER AND PER HOUSEHOLD, 1999

Select Core-Based Statistical Areas (CBSAs) above Median Population

CBSA name	Top 20 areas by per-owner subsidy	
	Subsidy per owner-occupied unit	Subsidy per household
San Francisco-San Mateo-Redwood City, CA Metropolitan Division	$26,385	$13,327
San Jose-Sunnyvale-Santa Clara, CA Metropolitan Statistical Area	$24,629	$14,874
Bridgeport-Stamford-Norwalk, CT Metropolitan Statistical Area	$17,418	$12,075
Santa Barbara-Santa Maria-Goleta, CA Metropolitan Statistical Area	$16,759	$9,593
Suffolk County-Nassau County, NY Metropolitan Division	$15,655	$12,520
Oakland-Fremont-Hayward, CA Metropolitan Division	$15,151	$9,189
New York-Wayne-White Plains, NY-NJ Metropolitan Division	$14,776	$6,123
Santa Ana-Anaheim-Irvine, CA Metropolitan Division	$14,593	$8,953
Salinas, CA Metropolitan Statistical Area	$14,554	$7,994
Honolulu, HI Metropolitan Statistical Area	$14,115	$7,944
Santa Rosa-Petaluma, CA Metropolitan Statistical Area	$13,030	$8,338
Oxnard-Thousand Oaks-Ventura, CA Metropolitan Statistical Area	$12,895	$8,734
Cambridge-Newton-Framingham, MA Metropolitan Division	$12,643	$7,804
Los Angeles-Long Beach-Glendale, CA Metropolitan Division	$12,096	$5,845
Boulder, CO Metropolitan Statistical Area	$11,855	$7,719
San Diego-Carlsbad-San Marcos, CA Metropolitan Statistical Area	$11,641	$6,476
Bethesda-Frederick-Gaithersburg, MD Metropolitan Division	$11,223	$7,894
Boston-Quincy, MA Metropolitan Division	$10,941	$6,389
Newark-Union, NJ-PA Metropolitan Division	$10,870	$6,823
Lake County-Kenosha County, IL-WI Metropolitan Division	$10,700	$8,127

continued on next page

Table 5-2 continued

| CBSA name | Bottom 20 areas by per-owner subsidy, 1999 | |
	Subsidy per owner-occupied unit	Subsidy per household
McAllen-Edinburg-Pharr, TX Metropolitan Statistical Area	$1,541	$1,126
Brownsville-Harlingen, TX Metropolitan Statistical Area	$1,696	$1,149
Beaumont-Port Arthur, TX Metropolitan Statistical Area	$2,027	$1,428
El Paso, TX Metropolitan Statistical Area	$2,153	$1,380
Lubbock, TX Metropolitan Statistical Area	$2,326	$1,380
Corpus Christi, TX Metropolitan Statistical Area	$2,341	$1,483
Killeen-Temple-Fort Hood, TX Metropolitan Statistical Area	$2,345	$1,329
Huntington-Ashland, WV-KY-OH Metropolitan Statistical Area	$2,448	$1,765
Ocala, FL Metropolitan Statistical Area	$2,466	$1,969
Lakeland-Winter Haven, FL Metropolitan Statistical Area	$2,528	$1,855
Fort Smith, AR-OK Metropolitan Statistical Area	$2,537	$1,785
Kingsport-Bristol, TN-VA Metropolitan Statistical Area	$2,789	$2,136
Deltona-Daytona Beach-Ormond Beach, FL Metropolitan Statistical Area	$2,866	$2,162
Shreveport-Bossier City, LA Metropolitan Statistical Area	$2,873	$1,901
San Antonio, TX Metropolitan Statistical Area	$2,931	$1,891
Pensacola-Ferry Pass-Brent, FL Metropolitan Statistical Area	$3,000	$2,134
Youngstown-Warren-Boardman, OH-PA Metropolitan Statistical Area	$3,069	$2,275
Charleston, WV Metropolitan Statistical Area	$3,071	$2,272
Mobile, AL Metropolitan Statistical Area	$3,087	$2,158
Scranton-Wilkes-Barre, PA Metropolitan Statistical Area	$3,156	$2,199

SOURCE: Sinai and Gyourko 2004.
NOTE: Median number of households in 1999 among all 380 CBSAs is 92,249.

lowest subsidy amounts per owner. Places with high average incomes, tax rates, and house prices clearly receive much greater benefit from the tax code subsidy to homeownership.

While this program is very large in economic terms, the home mortgage interest deduction on its own cannot have made housing more affordable for most modest-income owners anywhere in the country. This is because there literally are no tax shelter benefits to homeowners who do not itemize on their federal tax returns. Using data from the latest Survey of Consumer Finances (SCF), Poterba and Sinai (2008) report that most owners itemize, but there is a huge variation in the rate by income. The study estimates that while 63 percent of all owners itemize, only 23 percent of those with incomes below $40,000 do, versus 98 percent for those with incomes above $125,000. Simply put, those who do not itemize are net losers under this program to the extent that they bear any of the costs of financing the subsidy to those who do itemize.

Other features of the tax code's treatment of housing have more of an impact on lower-income Americans. For example, any homeowner who sells a house benefits from the fact that the capital gains on the home are not taxed. Even in this case, however, the benefits do not accrue evenly across the population. The lack of a capital gains tax on housing appreciation surely benefits richer owners with more valuable homes.

Whether the tax shelter benefits accruing to owners who do itemize make owning a home cheaper depends critically on whether owners actually retain the tax benefits or effectively transfer them to the seller by bidding up the house price with the added resources from the subsidy. If buyers of homes end up transferring the subsidy to those who sold them the home by bidding up the purchase price by the amount of the tax-code-related benefits, then the subsidy actually doesn't make housing any cheaper for new buyers. In this case, the home mortgage interest deduction just creates a one-time transfer to existing homeowners.

For those familiar with microeconomics, the question of who really benefits from the subsidy is a question of the incidence of the subsidy, which can be answered with the simple graphs discussed below. For the vast majority who do not like economics as much as we do, the answer to the question of who really benefits from this subsidy is determined by whether the buyer or seller of the home is in the best position to keep it. How do you ensure that you reap the benefits of the subsidy in this case? By having something that is very scarce and in high demand—say, a house for sale in an attractive, productive market like San Francisco in which local regulation severely limits the building of any new competitive homes. If there are many potential demanders competing for your scarce house, you can receive the full benefits of the subsidy through a higher purchase price. If that happens, the subsidy is said to be capitalized into the house price to the benefit of the seller.

Note that this means that the party actually benefiting from the subsidy need not be the party that the tax code says receives it. The statutory language determines what is called the legal incidence of the subsidy, and it clearly falls on the buyer of the home in this case, because that is who will deduct mortgage interest and local property taxes while occupying it. However, economic incidence, which is defined by the party that actually benefits from the subsidy, is determined by the economic realities of the marketplace. These realities have nothing to with the statutory language that created the subsidy. In other words, legal incidence is irrelevant to the economic incidence of a subsidy, which means that one cannot simply look to the law to determine who really benefits.

Let us consider two cases that define the boundaries of how this particular subsidy influences housing affordability in different types of markets. One case involves a market like San Francisco that has very high prices, signaling that demand is very strong, but that also permits very little new construction. With average house prices now well over $700,000, this market still has issued barely more than four thousand housing permits per year on average since 1980.[5] The other involves a market like Atlanta in which prices are much more modest and new construction is plentiful. Average house prices were well under $200,000 as of late 2007, while over forty thousand permits were issued annually on average since 1980.[6]

In San Francisco, sellers of homes possess the scarce good that is in high demand. There are many buyers wanting to live in the region, but sellers face relatively little competition from new housing units. Hence, competition among buyers for the scarce sites in San Francisco leads them to transfer the tax-code-related subsidy to sellers by bidding up the purchase price of the home. Graphically, this situation is depicted in figure 5-1. In this figure, the supply of housing is almost perfectly vertical, reflecting the fact that few permits are issued to allow new homes to be brought to the market, even as

FIGURE 5-1

INCIDENCE AND INELASTIC SUPPLY

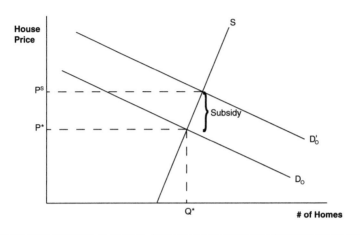

SOURCE: Authors' illustration.

prices become very high.[7] Demand for housing is given by the D_0 schedule, and the familiar intersection of supply and demand yields the price and quantity of housing in the market, P^* and Q^*, respectively.

A new subsidy to homeowners in this market will push their gross-of-subsidy demand higher. This increased demand is shown by the D'_0 curve in the figure. The size of the subsidy is reflected in the vertical distance between D_0 and D'_0. When housing supply is constrained, housing prices rise to P^s, so that almost the full amount of the subsidy shows up in higher prices.[8]

In this case, the original owner at the time the subsidy program was introduced reaps virtually all the program benefits. For our purposes, the important implication is that this very large subsidy program is not making housing more affordable in markets with supply and demand conditions like those depicted in figure 5-1. Those buyers who are able to take advantage of the home mortgage interest deduction will see their benefits vanish into the higher prices they have to pay for homes. Those buyers who don't itemize will find housing strictly less affordable, since housing prices have risen and they haven't been able to enjoy any offsetting benefit.

We do not know exactly the differences in the elasticity of housing supply across different markets, but the available data, including that from the
recent Wharton survey discussed in the previous chapter, strongly suggest
that the most inelastic markets are on the coasts. High prices and low permitting are the hallmarks of communities with inelastic housing supply.
Communities that combine those two characteristics are concentrated all
along the West Coast and from Washington, D.C., to Boston, MA, along the
East Coast. Not only are these markets physically constrained in terms of
land area because they border the Atlantic or Pacific oceans, but they have
stringent regulations that restrict the ability of homebuilders to supply new
units to the market.[9] Gyourko and Sinai (2003) estimate that house prices
in these markets are about 20 percent higher on average because the
subsidy is capitalized into property values, and a few markets far exceed
that number.

However, not all housing markets severely restrict building; Atlanta, as
we indicated, allows plentiful new supply. Demand for Atlanta is strong, but
the competition from new supply leaves sellers of homes in this market in
no position to extract the subsidy from its legal owner, the purchaser. Figure 5-2 graphically depicts a housing market like Atlanta's. To hold every-
thing constant but supply, the initial demand (D_0) and gross-of-subsidy
demand (D'_0) are the same as in figure 5-1. However, the supply of housing is given by the flat schedule S in this market. Modest increases in prices
elicit substantial new production of housing, which is consistent with the
persistently high permitting levels in this market.[10]

As usual, the intersection of demand and supply tells us the initial
price and quantity. However, introducing the same subsidy in this more
elastically supplied market results in only a very slight increase in price
(from P^* to P^s), along with a large increase in the quantity of housing consumed (from Q^* to Q^1). The subsidy is not capitalized into higher prices
in this market, so home purchasers keep most of it. In these places, the tax-
code-related subsidy does make it cheaper to own one's home. The so-
called user cost of owning, which reflects all costs (including expected
capital gains) associated with occupying a house for a year, is lower here
than in our other market because the subsidy reduces the after-tax cost of
mortgage debt service and local property taxes—without causing house
prices to rise commensurately.

FIGURE 5-2

INCIDENCE AND ELASTIC SUPPLY

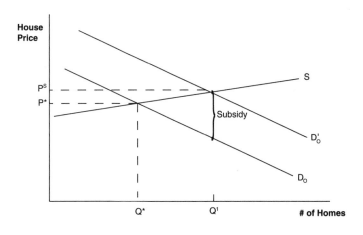

SOURCE: Authors' illustration.

The subsidy in this type of market stimulates the demand for housing and changes the behavior of different households. For example, it causes some households to own rather than rent. However, Glaeser and Shapiro (2003) have noted that the impact on the homeownership rate is small because the subsidy is targeted toward the rich, who would own even in its absence. A more important effect probably is on the quality of the home consumed, with people living in bigger and better homes than they would have otherwise. The majority of markets in the United States still have house prices fairly close to physical construction costs, which is consistent with a flat (or elastic) supply schedule (Glaeser, Gyourko, and Saks 2005), so this is the outcome expected for most interior markets in the country.

This analysis implies a number of important points regarding how this very large and costly subsidy program has affected housing affordability. First, the program cannot have made homeownership cheaper for any household that does not itemize on its federal tax return. Second, the price that non-itemizers have to pay to become owners can be significantly higher if they live in one of the nation's coastal markets with inelastic, or steeply sloped, supply sides to their housing markets. Thus, this program exacerbates, rather than mitigates, any housing affordability problems for this group of households. Third, the program does little or nothing to improve affordability conditions even for itemizers in supply-constrained markets. The bulk of the subsidy simply is transferred to existing owners via higher purchase prices. Obviously, this latter group of households does benefit, but why society would want to provide windfall capital gains to existing owners in markets that are deliberately restricting housing production is not at all clear to us. Almost certainly, this is an unintended, and largely unrecognized, consequence of the policy.[11] Fourth, there are many markets, primarily in the interior of the country, in which the user costs of owning are lower because of this subsidy program. Some of the households in these places own rather than rent, while others occupy higher-quality homes than they would in the absence of the subsidy. However, it is in precisely these markets where there is no fundamental affordability problem. Housing prices are not appreciably above physical production costs, so this program is not needed to solve a problem of underproduction in those markets.

While one can legitimately debate whether such a subsidy is justified if, for example, we assume that homeowners are better citizens, there is no doubt about whether this program has made housing more affordable. The answer is "no." Otherwise, San Francisco would be an affordable market, given the magnitudes of the subsidy flows involved.

We also question whether increasing housing consumption for homeowners is itself a worthy social goal. Increasing homeownership might be desirable, but why is it socially valuable to induce people to live in larger homes? In the old world of dumbbell apartments in dilapidated tenements, there may have been a case for government policies to improve housing quality and size. That case seems much harder to make in today's world of suburban McMansions.

Credit Market Interventions:
The Rise of Fannie Mae and Freddie Mac

Given that complex, extremely durable goods such as housing are expensive relative to current incomes, a sound, liquid, long-term mortgage market is critical to making homeownership financially accessible to the average household. That federal agencies have played an important role in the development of such a mortgage market is indisputable.

The Federal Home Loan Bank (FHLB) system, the first housing-related government-sponsored enterprise, was created in 1932 to provide a steady source of capital for member institutions struggling to deal with the surge in defaults that occurred during the Great Depression. Subsequently, the Federal National Mortgage Association, or Fannie Mae, and the Federal Home Loan Mortgage Corporation, or Freddie Mac, were created in 1968 and 1970, respectively, to provide added liquidity in the primary mortgage market and to help create a secondary market in which loans were securitized.[12]

The success of the primary mortgage market can be seen in the over $3 trillion in conventional single-family mortgages that were originated in 2005 alone, a figure that represents almost a ninefold increase from the volume issued in 1990. There is over $10 trillion in single-family mortgages outstanding, with a large share of them securitized by Fannie Mae, Freddie Mac, or private issuers (Office of Federal Housing Enterprise Oversight 2006a, 2006b). Prior to the recent crisis, bid-ask spreads on residential mortgage-backed securities typically were no wider than those on U.S. Treasuries. Indeed, many people have suggested that the current subprime crisis has arisen partly because the credit market was too ready to lend to poorer borrowers. Without debating the validity of such claims, we merely note that this represents a remarkable turnaround from even a few years ago, when lenders were overwhelmingly criticized for not lending to the poor.

Were this market to shrink considerably, as it might in the wake of the mortgage market crisis that now includes the federal takeover of Fannie Mae and Freddie Mac, there is no doubt that many households would have more difficulty owning a home. However, the relevant question for our analysis is whether the housing GSEs are necessary to the ongoing functioning of this market under normal conditions. That is, if capital markets were functioning well and the government decided to spin off Fannie Mae and Freddie Mac as private entities, would housing become fundamentally less affordable, or would private firms be able to provide similar mortgage liquidity at roughly the same interest rates? Stated differently, is there any evidence that Fannie Mae and Freddie Mac materially improved housing affordability for the typical household before the current credit crisis?

To answer this question, one first needs to know whether there really is a subsidy being provided to these entities because of their status as GSEs. Presuming the answer to that question is "yes" (and it is, as we show below), one then needs to know whether any of the subsidy is being passed along to home buyers via lower borrowing costs. If the answer to this second question is "yes," some actor in the housing market is benefiting, but we still need to perform an incidence analysis akin to that described above for the tax subsidy to homeownership in order to determine whether the subsidy is being passed through to consumers in a way that makes housing more affordable.

These questions have been the subject of much recent study, as regulation of the GSEs was debated prior to their takeover by the federal government. There is widespread agreement that the GSEs benefitted in various ways from their special status. The Congressional Budget Office (2001) concluded that Fannie Mae, Freddie Mac, and the FHLB system banks received $13.6 billion in subsidies in the year 2000, with the vast majority of that benefit arising from the implicit government backing of the debt issued by these entities. That guarantee allowed the GSEs to raise money more cheaply than comparable private firms. Two recent studies published in academic journals conclude that the housing GSEs have a twenty-five to seventy basis point advantage in terms of the cost of debt capital (Ambrose and Warga 2002; Nothaft, Pearce, and Stevanovic 2002).[13]

There also is general agreement that at least some of the benefit of being able to raise debt very cheaply was passed through to borrowers in the form of lower mortgage interest rates. For example, the Congressional Budget Office (2001) estimates that just over half of the subsidy to the GSEs was passed through to mortgage borrowers. And recent academic research suggests that mortgage interest rates on conforming loans are twenty to twenty-five basis points lower than they would be in the absence of the subsidy to the GSEs (Passmore, Sparks, and Ingpen 2002; McKenzie 2002).

The decline in monthly debt service from a reduction in interest rates of twenty-five basis points is a small amount for a typical mortgage. Consider a $250,000 home that is being financed with a $50,000 down payment equal to 20 percent of house value and a $200,000 fully amortizing, thirty-year mortgage with a fixed rate of 6.4 percent Such a home and mortgage are typical of the American housing market over the past five to ten years. The monthly debt service payment on that loan is $1,248. The monthly payment on a 6.15 percent rate mortgage, which is twenty-five basis points lower, is $1,215. This relatively small difference of $33 per month, or $396 per year, suggests the subsidy cannot be having a major impact on housing affordability, at least for the typical borrower.[14] This calculation also presumes that the lower debt service payments are not capitalized into land values and effectively passed along to the existing homeowner.

As in the case of the tax code subsidy to owners, we would expect extensive capitalization of these debt service savings into land prices in coastal markets with inelastic supplies of housing, and, in turn, little or no net benefits to home buyers in those places. The debt service savings probably are retained by home purchasers in markets with elastic supplies of housing, but these savings are modest, as illustrated by the calculation above. In those places with elastic housing supply, no shortage of housing or artificially high prices seem to warrant this type of policy intervention to lower the costs of being a homeowner.

Indeed, the best justification for an implicit subsidy to the GSEs is that they are solving a problem in the credit market, not a problem in the housing market. Prior to their takeover, many argued that Fannie Mae and Freddie Mac were needed to provide essential liquidity to an increasingly distressed home mortgage market. However, their ultimate failure demonstrated that their implicit (now explicit) subsidization came with potentially huge liabilities for taxpayers. Given the evidence that the housing GSEs have not contributed to substantially lower debt cost for borrowers, it would not be sound policy for the government to spin off Fannie Mae and Freddie Mac in anything like their previous forms. Until just before the demise of these companies, management and shareholders appear to have been reaping much of the benefit of the federal subsidy, with little offsetting gain in terms of housing affordability.[15]

Project-Based Subsidy Programs for the Development of Affordable Housing: Public Housing and Low Income Housing Tax Credit Programs

The home mortgage interest deduction and support for the credit markets can both be seen as what we have called demand-side subsidies for the housing market. We now turn to supply-side interventions, by which we mean those policies that subsidize the construction or rehabilitation of new homes.

The earliest supply-side interventions involved direct government provision of housing. Over time, the disappointing results of these public housing projects led to greater enthusiasm for using the tax code to support private development. While these private developments may avoid some of the worst problems of public housing construction, they seem to yield low social returns for large tax outlays. Moreover, the fact that these programs treat all markets more or less equally is particularly problematic. While it may make sense to subsidize housing in high-cost areas, it cannot make sense to subsidize new construction in areas where housing is already abundant and cheap.

For nearly three decades following passage of the Housing Act of 1937, the most prominent and important subsidized housing program involved the development and operation of publicly constructed and owned housing units. While public housing was owned and operated by local public housing authorities, the federal government paid for development costs, with tenants and local taxpayers responsible for operating costs. Beginning in 1968, the federal government introduced subsidies for operations in conjunction with new restrictions on the rents that could be charged. This period also saw the development of subsidies for modernization of public housing units in return for rent restrictions. Effectively, the 1970s saw the expansion of federal subsidies to cover some part of operations in return for increased targeting of very low-income households.

Olsen (2003) notes that there are over thirty-four hundred local public housing authorities in existence—that is, there are multiple such organizations within the typical metropolitan area. Public housing construction programs also were very large as late as 1980. In that year, funding commitments were authorized for nearly 130,000 new housing units, the vast majority of which were assisted through the public housing program (U.S. Congress 2004, table 15-23).[16]

There have been at least one million public housing units in existence since the early 1970s, with the size of the public housing stock peaking at just over 1.4 million units in 1991. Since then, following authorized demolitions and the decision not to rehabilitate some older units, the stock has dropped by well over one hundred thousand units. The data in table 5-3, from HUD's

TABLE 5-3

A PICTURE OF SUBSIDIZED HOUSEHOLDS, 2000

Name	Total units	% Occupied
U.S. Low Income Housing Tax Credit	945,347	90
U.S. Total Moderate Rehabilitation	111,392	65
U.S. Total Section 8 New Construction/ Substantial Rehab	877,830	84
U.S. Total Section 236	440,329	96
U.S. Total Multifamily/Other	352,337	98
U.S. Total Section 8 Certificates + Vouchers	1,817,360	82
U.S. Total Public Housing	1,282,099	89

SOURCE: HUD, Picture of Subsidized Households—2000.

Picture of Subsidized Households, 2000 (the latest year available), show less than 1.3 million public housing units in total, with 89 percent of them occupied. This represents only 23 percent of subsidized units that year. While not insignificant, public housing continues to shrink absolutely and relative to all subsidy programs.

The number of net new commitments has been under ten thousand units per year since 2000 (U.S. Congress 2004, table 15-23), which pales in comparison to the expansion of the Low Income Housing Tax Credit units, for which authorizations have been running in excess of seventy thousand annually. Demolitions of some of the bigger and older complexes are likely to continue to shrink the stock somewhat. Partly, this is due to the now widespread belief that concentrating large numbers of very poor households in high-rise structures is poor policy. The little purely public housing that is getting built is being kept on a small scale, so that poverty is more dispersed, not increasingly concentrated geographically.

Given the perceived failures of public housing, policymakers over the past two decades have tried to attract more private capital markets and construction expertise to help build affordable housing. This is now done primarily though the Low Income Housing Tax Credit program. The LIHTC was introduced in 1986 as part of the major tax reform act passed that year, and it rapidly grew into the largest project-based subsidy program. The

TABLE 5-4
STATISTICAL OVERVIEW OF THE LIHTC PROGRAM, 1987–2005

Year	Total allocated	Total units
1987	$62,885,954	34,491
1988	$209,779,916	81,408
1989	$307,182,516	126,200
1990	$213,148,840	74,029
1991	$400,420,875	111,970
1992	$337,032,273	91,300
1993	$424,701,977	103,756
1994	$494,914,237	117,099
1995	$420,922,941	86,343
1996	$378,920,852	77,003
1997	$382,894,328	70,453
1998	$368,077,833	67,822
1999	$374,670,775	62,240
2000	$378,749,319	59,601
2001	$462,426,235	67,261
2002	$524,379,530	69,310
2003	$572,121,789	73,877
2004	$605,786,677	75,600
2005	$612,605,239	70,630
Total	$7,531,622,106	1,520,393

SOURCE: Danter Company 2008.

LIHTC has become a significant influence in the nation's rental market. From 1995 through 2004, just over one-third of all privately owned multi-family units were built with governmental support.[17]

Under the LIHTC program, the federal government annually provides a certain number of tax credits to each state. The number is determined by a formula linked to the state's population. The states then distribute the credits to developers. The program was recently expanded, and table 5-4 lists the credits allocated since program inception in 1987, along with the number of housing units authorized (but not necessarily placed in service that year).[18]

For the developer, the LIHTC program provides a capital subsidy in the form of a stream of tax credits over ten years.[19] The tax credits must be used for the construction or rehabilitation of projects that meet two primary requirements: (a) projects must target low-income households using one of two formulas; the first is that at least 20 percent of the units in the project must be rent restricted (as described below) *and* occupied by people whose incomes are no more than 50 percent of the metropolitan area median income; the alternative is for at least 40 percent of the units to be rent restricted *and* occupied by people whose incomes are not more than 60 percent of the area median;[20] and (b) projects receiving tax credits must stay eligible for thirty years.[21]

As Baum-Snow and Marion (2008) have emphasized, another feature of the LIHTC is that tax credits increase by as much as 30 percent for units that are developed in "qualified census tracts." A census tract becomes "qualified" if it has a poverty rate above 25 percent or if more than 50 percent of its households have incomes below 60 percent of the area median gross income. Baum-Snow and Marion show that the increased subsidy that comes from locating in high-poverty areas does increase the tendency of LIHTC projects to locate in particularly poor areas. We will discuss the adverse economic consequences of this policy later.

The rent restriction on all LIHTC units is based on a 30 percent rule, but that rule applies to an administratively determined maximum eligible income for the area, not each individual household's income. Rents are capped at 30 percent of the maximum eligible income. The incomes themselves are posted by HUD each year. Income for a family of four serves as the base, with adjustments for larger or smaller families[22] and for county of residence. At its simplest, the amount equal to one-half of the area median is labeled the Very Low Income level for a family of four.

For example, in Franklin County, which is the core county of the Columbus, OH, metropolitan area, HUD determined that the median income for a four-person family in 2005 was $64,000, implying that the Very Low Income level for the same-size family was $32,000. The situation is more complicated in some other places, because HUD adjusts the Very Low Income level up to account for high housing costs and hard-to-develop tracts. This is relevant in San Francisco County, for example, where HUD's median income level for a four-person family was $95,000 in 2005, while its Very Low Income level for that county was $56,550 (which is 60 percent of the area median and is the highest Very Low Income amount for any county that year).[23]

Overall rents in LIHTC projects, including those for restricted and unrestricted units, typically are no more than 18 percent of the area median income (i.e., $0.3 \times 0.6 = 0.18$), although this can vary a bit because HUD makes adjustments up and down for household size. For Columbus, OH, this means that monthly rents in 2005 were about $960 for a family of four earning 60 percent of the Franklin County median. The analogous figure for a four-person family in San Francisco is $1,697. Rents like these would apply to three- to four-bedroom units in qualified LIHTC projects in each city.[24] Since rents are restricted to 30 percent of the maximum eligible income, subsidized tenants who earn less than that maximum must be paying more than 30 percent of their incomes.

While the formal program rules require only one-fifth to two-fifths of the units in a LIHTC project to be rent restricted and occupied by someone earning no more than 50 to 60 percent of the area median, in practice the vast majority of units built under the program are rented to tenants earning no more than 60 percent of the area median income. HUD data show that the fraction of units serving families earning below the Very Low Income threshold have ranged from the mid–80 percent level to the high–90 percent level over the past two decades. Research by Cummings and DiPasquale (1999, table 5) suggests that LIHTC project tenants tend to have incomes in the range of 40 to 60 percent of area medians.

The high concentration of low-income residents in LIHTC projects occurs because the states distributing the tax credits favor projects with more units subject to income and rent restrictions. The tax credits themselves are valuable enough that developers want high numbers of low-income families in order to maximize the credits received. The incentive to locate the projects in high-poverty areas also surely increases the share of poorer tenants in the subsidized buildings. Returns are sufficiently high to generate a long queue of developers, with Olsen (2003) noting that developers have been proposing projects that would require three times the amount of LIHTC funds allocated to the states by the federal government.

Putting these figures together, we see the typical LIHTC unit tenant: someone earning about one-half of the area median income who is paying

TABLE 5-5

TAX CREDIT ALLOCATIONS, 1987–2005

State[a]	Population 2005	Total allocations 1987–2005	Total units 1987–2005
California	36,132,147	$932,447,467	115,478
Texas	22,859,968	$500,710,062	159,296
New York	19,254,630	$554,276,534	73,397
Florida	17,789,864	$424,916,761	85,024
Illinois	12,763,371	$321,028,502	57,180
Pennsylvania	12,429,616	$313,325,531	52,850
Ohio	11,464,042	$306,524,684	72,039
Michigan	10,120,860	$276,558,314	57,497
Georgia	9,072,576	$196,056,434	53,065
New Jersey	8,717,925	$229,532,248	27,275
North Carolina	8,683,242	$176,455,103	40,034
Virginia	7,567,465	$198,669,724	48,775
Massachusetts	6,398,743	$181,955,993	29,936
Washington	6,287,759	$154,555,074	27,127
Indiana	6,271,973	$158,616,976	33,362
Tennessee	5,962,959	$128,130,720	33,290
Arizona	5,939,292	$125,848,916	21,514
Missouri	5,800,310	$138,784,665	32,318
Maryland	5,600,388	$143,407,560	31,631
Wisconsin	5,536,201	$144,984,708	33,220
Minnesota	5,132,799	$125,082,935	27,081
Colorado	4,665,177	$105,459,497	17,777
Alabama	4,557,808	$107,780,897	28,187
Louisiana	4,523,628	$122,715,167	40,204
South Carolina	4,255,083	$102,585,344	25,065
Kentucky	4,173,405	$112,126,768	25,992
Oregon	3,641,056	$87,381,812	17,594
Oklahoma	3,547,884	$78,325,513	26,627
Connecticut	3,510,297	$92,711,858	11,412
Iowa	2,966,334	$74,638,565	17,792
Mississippi	2,921,088	$69,587,209	23,643
Arkansas	2,779,154	$60,333,578	17,545
Kansas	2,744,687	$77,782,511	20,545

continued on next page

Table 5-5 continued

State	Population 2005	Total allocations 1987–2005	Total units 1987–2005
Utah	2,469,585	$60,112,806	12,807
Nevada	2,414,807	$45,707,575	9,149
New Mexico	1,928,384	$48,098,533	10,454
West Virginia	1,816,856	$38,897,395	9,876
Nebraska	1,758,787	$46,743,188	10,151
Idaho	1,429,096	$31,656,945	7,056
Maine	1,321,505	$31,720,272	5,708
New Hampshire	1,309,940	$25,504,591	3,833
Hawaii	1,275,194	$30,266,470	3,709
Rhode Island	1,076,189	$34,281,120	6,277
Montana	935,670	$21,986,702	4,099
Delaware	843,524	$25,711,168	6,080
South Dakota	775,933	$22,690,034	6,366
Alaska	663,661	$18,824,979	2,299
North Dakota	636,677	$24,115,043	5,132
Vermont	623,050	$22,151,103	4,498
District of Columbia	550,521	$12,755,465	6,150
Wyoming	509,294	$18,553,890	3,349

SOURCE: Danter Company 2006.
NOTE: a. Plus the District of Columbia.

about 18 percent of the area median income in rent. People who were much poorer than this would not be able to afford even the LIHTC-subsidized rents. Extra subsidies beyond tax credits are often needed to make LIHTC units accessible to the poorest Americans.[25] This fact only reinforces the point made earlier about the very poor needing more resources in general. Even the very large subsidies involved in the LIHTC program cannot make housing readily accessible for the most disadvantaged, and building more units does not address their underlying resource constraint.

Another defect of the LIHTC program is that it subsidizes construction across the country, even in markets where the unsubsidized private sector offers plentiful new supply and no affordability problems exist. This is because the tax credits are allocated to each state largely on the basis of population. The three columns of table 5-5 report estimated state populations in 2005, total tax credit allocations to each state from program inception in 1987 through 2005, and total housing units funded over the same time period.[26] While population is the prime driver of allocations, it clearly is not the only determinant of housing units funded, as a comparison of California and Texas illustrates.

California has a much larger population and has received almost double the credits allocated to Texas. However, Texas has 38 percent more units under the program. Obviously, California's average allocation per housing unit is much larger. One reason for this is that housing costs tend to be much higher in many parts of California. Another is that the state officials in Texas responsible for running their program tend to be more aggressive in finding ways to use their credits to fund a larger number of projects and units. While there is variation in the intensity of LIHTC production across states, this variation occurs because of cost differences and the preferences of state officials, not simply because some areas need help with housing supply more than others.

Within markets, the Qualified Census Tract program ensures that LIHTC projects tend to be sited in poorer areas. A study of the program's first ten years (Cummings and DiPasquale 1999) found that in a sample of six market areas, less than 3 percent of LIHTC projects were located in census tracts with median incomes at or above the area-wide median.[27] Eriksen and Rosenthal (2007) report similar albeit less striking results. This study found that 56 percent of LIHTC projects are located in census tracts that have median incomes in the lower third of the distribution for their metropolitan area. Another 28 percent are in tracts with incomes from the middle third of their metropolitan distribution, leaving 16 percent located in tracts with median incomes in the upper third of their Metropolitan Statistical Area income distribution.

Baum-Snow and Marion (2008) also document that LIHTC rental units are much more likely to be located in poorer areas. Between 1990 and 2000, nearly half of the growth in apartments in tracts with half the households eligible for rent subsidies was subsidized by the LIHTC program, versus only 10 percent in higher-income tracts with 40 percent or less of households eligible for subsidies. Thus, recent evidence shows somewhat more production in higher-income tracts, but Cummings and DiPasquale's (1999, 303) characterization of the program as one that provides "better housing in poorer neighborhoods rather than housing opportunities for poor households in higher-income neighborhoods" still is largely accurate.

Cummings and DiPasquale (1999) also report on the correlation of LIHTC projects with previous residential construction activity in the census tract. Particularly in central cities, a good-sized fraction of LIHTC projects was being built in areas with little or no other construction activity (at least in the first decade of the program's existence). For example, 10 percent of LIHTC projects constructed in central cities were in census tracts that had had no new residential construction of any kind in the five years preceding the 1990 census. Just over one-quarter (27 percent) of the projects in central cities were in tracts with no rental construction in the preceding five years.

The cross-metropolitan area uniformity of the LIHTC is problematic because housing supply problems are more severe in some places than in others. The within-metropolitan heterogeneity in the location of LIHTC projects is also problematic because the program appears to be driving housing to the areas where it is valued least. A great advantage of the market is that high prices tell suppliers which goods are valued most. By responding to price signals, suppliers take care of the parts of the market where demand is most quickly outstripping supply.

The value of responding to price signals is high for all goods markets, but it is particularly so for housing. Housing deficits across metropolitan areas are best addressed by delivering housing where housing prices are the highest. This will cater to the areas with strongest demand and do the most to make housing more affordable everywhere. After all, if housing is being supplied in more expensive areas, then this creates less pressure to gentrify less expensive areas.

In contrast, by directing housing to low-price areas where there is no other private construction, the LIHTC ensures that new construction will generate the least social surplus and the least impact on overall housing affordability. Building in census tracts with little demand, even within high-demand metropolitan areas, does little to make housing more affordable overall. And building subsidized housing for poor people in poor areas seems to be artificially inducing them to stay in places without much economic opportunity. This cannot be good policy and almost certainly is another example of an unfortunate unintended consequence.

This skepticism aside, to properly evaluate the LIHTC requires comparing the costs of the project with its returns, measured either by greater housing supply or improved affordability. The LIHTC program fails this test, too, as there is little doubt that the projects are expensive and that a significant portion of their benefits accrues to developers. The high returns to developers participating in LIHTC projects are evidenced by the steady excess demand to participate in the program, as there always is the alternative of doing purely private deals

Currently, multifamily construction deals that are done by (or joint ventured with) equity real estate investment trusts are priced to generate expected internal rates of return (IRRs) in the low teens. Cummings and DiPasquale (1999) estimated much higher IRRs in the early years of the program (25 percent or more), but a significant risk premium is to be expected for deals done under any new program. More recently, Eriksen (2007) concluded that investors used a discount rate of nearly 12 percent when valuing the decade-long stream of tax credits involved in this program.

Cummings and DiPasquale (1999) estimated a subsidy rate as a share of total development costs (which was defined as the sum of net equity invested in the project plus all debt on the project). Subsidies from all sources (federal tax credits, state and local governments, etc.) amounted to 68 percent of total development costs on the average unit.[28] More recently, the U.S. General Accounting Office (GAO) estimated the present value of per-unit development subsidies on tax-credit-financed units. The study's estimate of $52,790 per unit (in 1999 dollars) in metropolitan areas is the sum of the value of tax credits, any grants provided, and interest subsidies on below-market loans. This average masks substantial variation across markets, as the GAO estimated per-unit subsides of only $31,470 in the Dallas-Fort Worth area versus $111,780 in New York (U.S. General Accounting Office 2002).[29]

Given the roughly seventy thousand tax credit units authorized per annum in recent years, a $50,000 per-unit subsidy translates into an aggregate subsidy value of $3.5 billion per year. Hence, producing these units is not cheap, and the GAO study concludes that subsidizing production via tax credits is about 30 percent more expensive than a voucher program.[30]

We will return to the differences in costs across housing programs later in this chapter. We consider now how much net new housing actually gets built under the LIHTC program. Does production under the LIHTC program crowd out other housing that would have been built in its absence? Economists generally believe that subsidizing an activity increases the amount of that activity. But the LIHTC does not create a subsidy for all new building. The program provides a large subsidy to a select, small group of builders. If these builders would have built anyway, then subsidizing them makes little difference to the overall amount of construction.

Two recent studies that have asked whether subsidized housing production crowds out private development conclude that the answer is "yes" (Sinai and Waldfogel 2005; Eriksen and Rosenthal 2007). Sinai and Waldfogel (2005) examine subsidized production in general (not just LIHTC units) and estimate whether these programs result in more units after controlling as well as possible for other determinants of the demand for housing. The study finds a very large crowd-out effect of about two-thirds. That is, each unit of subsidized housing displaces about two-thirds of a purely private-sector unit, implying that the net increase in the housing stock is only one-third of the gross increase in units from the subsidy program.

Eriksen and Rosenthal (2007) focus exclusively on the LIHTC program and analyze more recent data. The study estimates a crowd-out effect of about 50 percent. This implies that the net annual increase in the housing stock from the delivery of 70,000 tax-credit-financed units each year is about thirty-five thousand apartments.[31] Another way to think about this in conjunction with program costs estimated in the GAO study is that there is about $100,000 in subsidies per net new housing unit due to the LIHTC.[32]

These studies are national in scope, while any crowd-out occurs within the context of a specific local housing market. Thus, the estimates in Sinai and Waldfogel (2005) and Eriksen and Rosenthal (2007) reflect an average of crowd-out across different markets. Their findings suggest that a significant amount of LIHTC unit production is occurring in markets that would have built much of this housing in the absence of the subsidy program (i.e., those markets with flat, or elastic, supplies of housing). Given the magnitude of the subsidies involved, this certainly makes the program look very wasteful.

The basic economics of housing markets helps us to understand why the LIHTC makes little sense in most of America. In areas with robust demand and highly elastic housing supply such as Houston or Atlanta, the LIHTC programs are far too small to make much of a difference to affordability and are substituting for much unsubsidized development that would have occurred anyway. If anything, the program serves only to ensure that there is development in those low-demand submarkets where housing probably shouldn't be built anyway.

In areas with weak demand and low housing prices, such as the declining inner cities of the Midwest, the LIHTC probably is adding to the housing stock. But given that housing prices are already quite low in these areas, why are we subsidizing housing there in the first place? There is no affordable housing problem in central city Cleveland or Buffalo. Their prices are well below, not above, construction costs. The affordability problem faced by their poor populations is much better dealt with via income transfers or vouchers. There is no need to intervene in their housing markets.

Only in the highly constrained areas along the East Coast and West Coast is it likely that the LIHTC is actually having much of an impact on supply. It is desirable to increase supply in these markets, so the best case for the LIHTC occurs in areas where housing prices are high and other types of supply are low. Nevertheless, we doubt that the LIHTC is a particularly efficient means of encouraging supply even in these areas where supply problems are most severe.

Our negative view of this program is only reinforced when we consider the impact on rents, which gets to the incidence of the subsidy. Because the LIHTC program subsidizes only a select group of the suppliers of housing, determining who really benefits from the subsidy is more complicated than determining who benefits from tax-code-related subsidies to homeowners.[33] Given reasonable assumptions, including that there are both subsidized and unsubsidized builders in each market and that both types of builders use the same construction technology so that their production costs are the same, it is likely that rents are no lower than they would be in the absence of the program. The demanders of the apartment units receive little or no benefit from the program, with the subsidized builders making higher profits and some unsubsidized firms being squeezed out of the market.[34]

In sum, the long queue of multifamily builders wishing to participate in the LIHTC program is easily understood: LIHTC essentially functions as a transfer program to them. Unfortunately, from both the average taxpayer's and low-income household's perspectives, there are precious few positive spillovers from the program in terms of net new production or lower rents. In our final chapter, which looks to a new housing policy, these flaws will lead us to recommend the complete elimination of the LIHTC program.

Tenant-Based Subsidies for the Consumption
of Affordable Housing: Section 8 Vouchers

Two major housing programs grew out of disappointment with public housing projects. The LIHTC was one, and Section 8 housing vouchers were the other. While various aspects of the voucher program certainly are debatable, we believe that it is the most successful of the federal government's housing programs. In-kind grants, or vouchers, are now the largest housing subsidy program as measured by the number of households involved (not by dollar budget). We are sympathetic to the view that cash is preferable to in-kind transfers, but if we are going to subsidize the housing of the poor, then vouchers are preferable to all the existing alternatives.

Housing vouchers have been used since 1974, when the Section 8 Existing Housing Program was authorized.[35] This so-called certificate program provided funds for poor households to rent units approved by the local housing authority. Standards for the program were imposed on both tenants and units. Tenants had to meet HUD's Very Low Income eligibility standard, which meant that the household had to earn less than 50 percent of the relevant area median (with adjustments for family size, as described above). The housing units had to meet habitability standards and have rents that were less than a so-called fair market rent (FMR), which presently is set at the 45th percentile of the local area rent distribution. In 1983, a separate voucher program was authorized that was different from the certificate program in two important ways: it allowed tenants to keep the savings if they could find a habitable unit that cost less than the FMR, and it permitted them to live in a unit renting for more than the FMR if they were willing to pay the difference. Today's voucher program essentially allows poorer households earning less than half the median income in an area to rent something close to the median apartment in their area, without having to spend more than 30 percent of their own income in the process.

These programs operated simultaneously until 1998, when they were consolidated. Throughout the remainder of this section, we refer to tenant-based subsidies as "vouchers," because treating the certificate and voucher programs as identical is acceptable for our purposes. As table 5-3 documents, vouchers now serve more households—over 1.8 million as of

2000—than any other subsidy program in existence. And, as noted above, they are cheaper than existing project-based subsidies for construction.

To provide some idea of the range of subsidies involved, it is useful to reconsider the Columbus, OH, and San Francisco, CA, markets discussed above in connection with the LIHTC program. Recall that the Very Low Income level cutoff for a family of four was $32,000 in Columbus and was $56,550 in San Francisco. Fair market rents in 2007 for a three-bedroom unit (which is appropriate for this size household) are $848 in Columbus and $2,071 in San Francisco.[36] With households expected to pay 30 percent of their incomes in rent, the four-person family in Columbus earning $32,000 would be expected to contribute $800 per month ($800 = ~0.3 × 32,000/12), so the implied subsidy would be only $48 per month. The family at the Very Low Income level cutoff in San Francisco would receive a larger subsidy. Thirty percent of that family's income is $16,965, implying a required payment of $1,414 per month. HUD would make up the $557 difference between the $2,071 fair market rent and the $1,414 the family would have to pay out of pocket.[37]

Naturally, HUD needs to make much larger expenditures for poorer households earning significantly less than the Very Low Income cutoff. This is the case even in a modestly priced market such as Columbus, OH. Consider a family earning 25 percent of that area's local median income. In Columbus, this is exactly one-half the Very Low Income cutoff, or $16,000 ($16,000 = 0.5 × $32,000). Thirty percent of that income level is only $4,800, so this family would be required to pay $400 per month toward the $848 rent on a three-bedroom unit. Thus, more than half the fair market rent must be subsidized for this family in Columbus. In San Francisco, a four-person household earning one quarter of the local area median would be responsible for only $594 of the $2,071 fair market rent for a three-bedroom apartment in that market. In this case, over two-thirds of the rent must be subsidized. In this way, vouchers are able to reach further down the income distribution than other programs and subsidize poorer households than are typically able to occupy units financed by tax credits.

Of course, since legal and economic incidence need not be the same, we need to investigate more carefully whether the tenants receiving vouchers actually keep the benefit of the subsidy. As suggested by the analysis above, it is possible that if tenants bid up rents in their market, they do not keep the full benefit. One recent study of the voucher program concludes that in areas where vouchers are more abundant, rents on units occupied by lower-income households have increased more than elsewhere (Susin 2002). More specifically, this work found that vouchers raised rents by 16 percent on average across ninety large metropolitan areas.[38]

However, other research dating back to the Housing Assistance Supply Experiment of the 1970s and 1980s suggests that the price impacts of vouchers are minimal. This strand of research emphasizes that offering vouchers increases the demand for distinct housing units only to the extent that the recipients were homeless or living with another family in a single apartment. The vast majority of families offered vouchers already live in a housing unit. Thus, the primary impact of vouchers should be to increase the demand for units that meet the program's quality standards and to decrease the demand for units that do not. This further suggests that the primary supply response is an upgrading of existing units to meet minimum program quality standards, not the building of new units.

Lowry's (1983) analysis of the Housing Assistance Supply Experiment indicates that these changes in the nature of the housing stock do, indeed, occur and that they happen fairly quickly. More recent work by Kennedy and Finkel (1994) on the Section 8 program confirms that many voucher recipients do occupy units that were brought up to standards after failing an initial inspection.

In general, this research suggests that the primary impact of the housing voucher program is to decrease demand for the lowest-quality housing and to increase demand for units of modest to average quality. This is inconsistent with Susin's (2002) finding that rents are higher for units at the bottom end of the quality distribution. However, the results from the Housing Assistance Supply Experiment, which show very small effects on rents from larger voucher issuance, possibly can be attributed to the location of the experiment in markets with flat (or elastic) supplies of housing. One would expect small price effects in those markets in any event.[39]

One concern about housing vouchers is that they do not sufficiently enable poorer people to leave poorer areas. We worried above that the LIHTC tended to locate projects in poorer areas and thereby reduced the tendency of the poor to move to better neighborhoods. The tenant-based voucher program does not restrict neighborhood choice, and this is one of its many virtues relative to the LIHTC. However, since the voucher program is administered by local housing authorities, it can be difficult to take a housing voucher across metropolitan area borders. In principle, this type of mobility is possible, but in practice it seems to be difficult. Given that there is no benefit from artificially restricting the ability of poor people to leave poor areas, improving the portability of vouchers is greatly to be desired.

In sum, there is no doubt that vouchers are much less expensive per unit of housing than are production subsidies such as tax credits. However, the evidence is more mixed on whether vouchers push up rents. We are more comfortable with the results from the old Housing Assistance Supply Experiment, which suggest relatively small price effects, than with findings showing the opposite, because the supply experiment findings are consistent with the voucher program primarily functioning to change the demand for different types of housing. That said, Susin's (2002) finding that voucher recipients end up passing at least some of the benefit along to landlords by bidding up rents should caution all that even this program probably is not an unmitigated success. That vouchers would increase rents is most plausible in coastal areas with highly restricted (inelastic) supply sides to their housing markets.[40] In those areas, there is some increase in the overall demand for housing, without a commensurate increase in supply. In all cases, increasing demand without increasing supply is a recipe for higher prices (rents, in this case). Nevertheless, we still conclude that vouchers are the most successful and beneficial of all the major federal interventions in the housing market.

Conclusion:
Toward a New National Housing Policy

While much recent policy analysis of housing markets naturally focuses on the fallout from the subprime crisis, the provisions in the recently passed Housing and Economic Recovery Act of 2008 that address the two distinct affordability issues facing the poor and middle class do not leave us optimistic that policymakers have learned much from past mistakes. There is a temporary increase in the amount of tax credits, but no reforms that would make the program more efficient or more likely to benefit low-income renters. In addition, a new national Housing Trust Fund is established, with the financing out of the housing GSEs' profits. Initially, the fund was intended to cover costs of defaulted loans from an FHA foreclosure program. Subsequently, the fund would have been used to build and rehabilitate affordable housing for low-income households. While that will not happen now that Fannie and Freddie have been taken over, the premise that these GSEs were part of the solution and not part of the problem shows how misguided policy prescriptions were well into 2008.

The basic plan of these programs seems likely to repeat the worst mistakes of past housing history. There is little reason to believe that the fund will be any more successful than the LIHTC in actually generating new units, rather than just subsidizing units that would have been produced anyway. Nor is there much reason to think that the fund will actually target resources toward the areas where housing supply is constrained.

While we are critical of these proposals, and indeed of much of federal housing policy, we do believe that the federal government should have a vigorous policy to promote affordable housing. Good policy first requires a sound diagnosis of the problems that need to be addressed. This volume

119

has emphasized that there are two quite different affordability problems, and that they require different public policy responses. The first is one of poverty. Housing, like cars and health care, is expensive for poorer Americans everywhere. For the truly disadvantaged, housing costs remain high even in Texas markets such as San Antonio and Dallas where prices are quite close to construction costs, as well as in central city Detroit where house prices are far below construction costs. The affordability problem facing poor people does not reflect any failure of the housing market, but rather their general lack of resources.

The second affordability problem that Americans face does reflect failures of the housing market. As we have shown, housing prices in a growing number of markets have moved further and further away from construction costs, making housing less and less affordable for middle-income Americans, not just the poor. These high-cost areas combine high demand and limited supply. We see the limited supply levels in construction figures that have declined steadily over time. The lack of supply in these high-cost regions is due mainly to land-use regulation that has made it difficult to build. As many localities have turned preventing new construction into an art form, there are now many areas unaffordable even to middle-income people.

Given this diagnosis, two very different policy responses are required. For the first affordability problem, the appropriate treatment is to give the poor the resources that society wants them to have. We prefer straightforward income transfers, but housing vouchers are the way to go if in-kind subsidies are required for political reasons. Solving this affordability problem does not require major changes to the housing market, and subsidy programs that focus on the supply side, such as the LIHTC, are not useful ways to address this issue. It makes no more sense to subsidize real estate developers to produce cheap housing for the poor than it would to subsidize auto companies to build a line of inexpensive cars for the poor. And if we must have a National Affordable Housing Trust Fund, the best use of its funds would be to provide more Section 8 vouchers, not build subsidized housing units.

To address the middle-class affordability issue, we must aim specifically at the failure of the housing market to deliver a sufficient supply of new units, a failure that helps keep prices high. The solution must target increasing supply in these constrained markets. Few national politicians or policy analysts have yet focused on this problem, so there is little track record for any national response to inefficiently stringent local land-use regulation. We attempt in this chapter to offer one. Readers may agree or disagree with the specifics of our proposal, for there always is much to debate in any serious housing policy. What we do insist on is that America needs different housing policies in different markets.

The Growing Affordability Problem in Markets with High Land Costs

The middle-class affordability problem, which is characterized by housing prices greatly exceeding construction costs, is not national in scope. Not yet, at least. As we have shown, the growing Sunbelt metropolitan areas such as Houston or Atlanta have housing prices that are generally close to construction costs, and much of the Rustbelt is even more affordable. It is the metropolitan areas along the West Coast, most of the markets from Washington, DC, to Boston, MA, some places in Hawaii, and the odd interior market that are still experiencing an affordability crisis.

Prices are much higher than construction costs in these areas because housing supply is insufficient relative to strong demand. As long as supply remains limited and demand for these places is robust, these areas will not become more affordable. Additional supply of all quality types, not just low-income housing, is the only real solution to this affordability problem in these markets. The typical number of units provided by any federal program is too small to make a meaningful difference for overall affordability in the high-cost areas. A few hundred, or even a few thousand, extra units will have little impact on housing supply in a larger metropolitan area. Only the private sector will be able to create enough housing to meaningfully push prices down. The key question is what government policies will prod the private sector into large-scale production in high-cost areas.

Fortunately, the defining attribute of high-cost areas—prices that are substantially above construction costs—itself virtually defines profitability for new building. Any builder who is able to construct a few hundred units in Silicon Valley or suburban Boston and sell them for two (or more) times construction costs would surely love to do so. Thus there is no need to subsidize developers to build in these markets. Their high house prices already make construction profitable enough.

Of course, if high prices in these markets really provided strong enough incentives for developers to build, we wouldn't see the current dearth of supply. As we have argued throughout, the combination of low construction levels and high prices is best understood as the result of land-use regulations that make it difficult and costly to build.[1] We see these rules as a classic politically induced market failure. When individual localities restrict housing supply, they are trying to improve the lives of a majority of their homeowners by reducing crowding and eliminating the inconvenience of new construction. At the same time, they are imposing costs on every prospective home buyer outside of that jurisdiction, who faces higher prices because of this limit on supply.[2]

Our core recommendation is that the federal government induce localities to ease the barriers to new construction that they have themselves created and that make housing unaffordable. We further recommend that the primary demand-side policy aimed at affordability for middle-income Americans, the home mortgage interest deduction, should be reformed in high-cost areas where housing is not elastically supplied.

Because our reform affects both the demand and supply sides of the housing market, it is useful to address the strengths and weaknesses of demand- and supply-side policies. In general, demand-side policies are easier to implement and monitor than supply-side policies. The benefits of the home mortgage interest deduction go directly to taxpayers, so there is no chance that they can be subverted by politically connected firms or used to fund white elephant projects. Housing vouchers are slightly more random and require more government bureaucracy, but the bulk of the spending on housing vouchers actually goes to pay for the housing costs of lower-income individuals.

In contrast, supply-side policies involve a great deal of discretion on the part of those administering them and make possible a great deal of waste and, possibly, fraud and corruption. We have no reason to believe that the Low Income Housing Tax Credit is poorly administered, but we have every reason to think that this program ends up enriching some developers and leading to many projects that should never have been built. Hence, we prefer demand-side to supply-side policies, all else equal.

All else is not equal in the markets with inelastic supplies of housing. Despite the innate disadvantages of supply-side policies, they still will be much more beneficial than subsidizing demand in these markets. Providing demand subsidies in these markets will not increase supply and thus will only further push up prices. This does suggest a natural fit between reforming current demand-side policies and creating a new supply-side policy in these markets. Given that the mortgage interest deduction results in even higher prices, it can be reduced without worsening affordability conditions in these supply-constrained markets. The revenues saved can be used to fund a supply-side program in the same markets. Linking these two reforms can therefore ensure a policy that is revenue neutral not just across the United States, but even within specific regions of the country.

One Size Does Not Fit All

We cannot overemphasize that solving the affordability problem for the middle class must concentrate on the places where the problem exists: the high-cost areas where new construction is quite limited and demand is strong. In the other areas of the country, wherever housing prices are either close to or below construction costs, the housing market is fundamentally working well. We should try to fix only those housing markets that are broken, and a housing market isn't broken if it is delivering homes at reasonable prices relative to construction costs.

More generally, basic economics and the best available research tell us that the relative merits of demand-side and supply-side policies depend upon how easy and flexible are supply conditions in each market. Recall what the economic incidence analysis in chapter 5 tells us: if supply conditions in a market are very flexible so that abundant new supply is forthcoming when prices rise even slightly, then a demand subsidy causes the quantity of housing to rise, but not the price. This is the best-case scenario for subsidies that are meant both to increase the consumption of housing and to benefit consumers while doing so. We may have doubts about using the tax code to encourage people to live in bigger homes, which the home mortgage interest deduction surely does in places with elastic housing supply, but at least the deduction doesn't act mainly to push up prices in those markets.

Conversely, when supply is very inflexible, the deduction acts mainly to increase prices. Housing is inelastically supplied in those tightly regulated markets that do not permit much new residential building. In this type of market, a demand-side subsidy causes prices to rise, but results in little or no change in the quantity of housing produced or consumed. In an intermediate case, in which there is a moderate degree of flexibility to housing supply, both consumers and suppliers benefit from a demand subsidy, as both the price and quantity of housing increase.[3]

Thus demand-side subsidies, which at least are not harmful and can be perfectly sensible in unregulated regions with highly elastic housing supply, tend to be counterproductive in tightly regulated markets where new housing supply is very limited. This is why the current demand-side approach can be sensible in Houston but not in San Jose. To repeat: one size does not fit all.

In reality, this story is not quite so simple, and for this reason: neither Section 8 vouchers nor the home mortgage interest deduction is truly a global demand subsidy. Vouchers are not mandated, so not all poor households receive them. The home mortgage interest deduction provides a subsidy only for those who both own their homes and itemize on their taxes. Thus these subsidies affect only a subsection of the market.

This nuance makes little difference in elastic markets such as Houston and Atlanta, where the subsidy does not increase price in any case. The impact of a limited subsidy in those markets is to increase consumption and provide benefits for the population that receives the subsidy, but it has little or no impact on prices or quantities for the population that does not directly receive it. In markets such as San Francisco or Boston that have inelastic supplies of housing, however, a limited subsidy affects both those who receive it and those who do not: the subsidy raises prices for everyone, and it causes the former to consume a greater share and the latter a lesser share of housing.

Thus, suppliers are not the only people who benefit from the demand subsidy in this case. The subsidized group also benefits, although this group's benefits will be less than the overall costs of the subsidy since the benefits are shared with suppliers. Importantly, the nonsubsidized group is made worse off by the subsidy since it faces higher prices with no offsetting subsidy, and there is likely to be a shift in housing consumption between the two groups: the subsidized buyers consume more and the unsubsidized buyers consume less housing than they would without the subsidy.[4]

This implies that there will be meaningful differences in the impacts of the home mortgage interest deduction versus Section 8 vouchers, even though both are demand-side policies. Thus, not only does one size not fit all, but not all subsidies have the same effects. Consider the users of the home mortgage interest deduction, who tend to be among the richest Americans (Glaeser and Shapiro 2003). In highly regulated markets that permit little new construction, the policy ends up redistributing from the poor to the rich because the poor, who do not itemize and take the standard deduction, have to pay higher home prices without receiving any subsidy. Consequently, if we wish to increase equity, it makes sense to reduce the home mortgage interest deduction in communities with inflexible (inelastic) housing supplies.

Users of Section 8 vouchers are disproportionately poor, so that even in inelastic communities, the voucher ensures that this group will consume more housing (albeit possibly by reducing the housing consumption of others). The voucher also will redistribute from rich to poor. While it surely makes sense to target vouchers toward more elastic areas, it probably does not make sense to eliminate them completely in communities with more inelastic housing supply, as doing so would make things less equitable. For this reason, we are more enthusiastic about reducing the home mortgage interest deduction in inelastic areas than we are about eliminating Section 8 vouchers in those same areas, especially if those vouchers are made fully portable across the nation.

Supply-side policies will also have a different impact in places with elastic and inelastic housing supply. While classic economic analysis suggests that the supply-side subsidies and demand-side subsidies are equivalent, this is not the case in the housing market, because the subsidy is to the builders, not the sellers, of homes.[5] The ultimate impact depends upon whether subsidies to new construction crowd out other building, and this will differ across regions of the country.

A classic supply-side intervention such as the LIHTC works to deliver specific subsidies to a small number of builders. If the supply of nonsubsidized new construction is perfectly elastic, as it appears close to being in many Sunbelt markets, then the impact of subsidized construction will be to completely crowd out an equivalent amount of nonsubsidized construction. It is in these markets that subsidizing new units is most wasteful, because there is no net change in the aggregate amount of housing units being produced (and no impact on price).

However, if the supply of nonsubsidized new construction is absolutely fixed in amount (perfectly inelastic), then any new units created by subsidization will add one-for-one to the housing stock. In this case, subsidizing supply will lead to an increase in the quantity of housing and a decrease in its price. But markets with little or no new supply, which are inelastic in nature, can have either strong or weak demand. Subsidizing supply makes no sense in declining markets that have little new construction, because they suffer from low demand. New construction in these areas just depresses prices even further, and it also leads to more people living in places where the economic future is bleak. It can hardly be in the national interest to artificially induce people to live in declining regions of the country. The best case for subsidizing new construction occurs in constrained markets where demand is high and local economies are strong.[6]

Can the Federal Government Induce Localities to Permit More Construction?

Perhaps the most straightforward way to increase construction in high-price areas would be to bar localities from excessively strict regulation of their land. Following the model of Massachusetts Chapter 40B, the federal government could subject communities with sufficiently high prices and sufficiently little new housing to zoning oversight by a national review board that was far more encouraging of new development than local boards. Such a plan could, at relatively little taxpayer expense, greatly increase the private supply of new development in the high-cost regions of the country. Of course, such a policy would run into both constitutional and administrative hurdles. We also are fairly confident that it would be wildly unpopular.

Another fairly draconian approach would simply be to cut off all federal aid to any communities where prices are high and new building is rare. Surely, this would create strong incentives for communities that don't build to rethink their zoning policies. We don't think that the time has yet come for such extreme measures. Still, this hypothetical illustrates how the federal government could use its current local aid to create very strong incentives for high-cost areas to permit more building. In principle, this type of policy could have a real impact on the middle-class affordability problem, and it wouldn't increase taxes.

Our proposal is a considerably more modest version that contains the same core idea: the federal government should lean against the local tendency to restrict new construction. Of course, land use has been under local control since the founding of the Republic, so it seems far-fetched simply to assume local control away. Moreover, there are good reasons to think that localities bring valuable information to the design of local land-use rules. We therefore recommend not eliminating local control, but using federal dollars to induce localities to be friendlier to new development.

Our simple program uses the extra tax revenue created by reforming the home mortgage interest deduction (discussed in detail below) to provide incentives that will induce overly restrictive communities (and only overly restrictive communities) to build. The program offers aid to localities in proportion to the amount of new construction they permit; if a supply-constrained community doubles the number of new units it builds, it doubles the amount of aid it receives. Since aid increases with the number of homes built, localities have incentives to permit more housing.[7]

While this middle-class affordability proposal does affect different regions in different ways, it applies a uniform standard across space so that as conditions change in a locale, the treatment of that locale will also change. Moreover, by funding this proposal with tax revenues generated by changes in the home mortgage interest deduction, we can ensure that it will be fiscally neutral across areas, and that total spending and tax benefits in each county will be held constant. We turn to the funding of the program later. At this point, we will just assume that there is federal aid that can be used to induce localities to build.

One alternative policy path would be to urge localities to adopt a model zoning code that would not allow the excessive regulation that discourages building. We have nothing against such zoning codes. Indeed, it might be sensible to encourage localities to adopt them in conjunction with our supply incentive program. However, we have enormous confidence in the ability of communities to slow down construction, no matter what the explicit rules on the books may be. Even if a community adopts a model code, it can still make the review process extremely difficult and find a host of objections to any project. Only by tying federal aid directly to the level of new building can we be sure that the aid will provide incentives for exactly the new construction that we are trying to elicit.

There still are three major questions that need to be answered if we are to create this program. First, how is the government to finance the program? Second, how is the program to decide which areas of the country are required to participate? Third, how is the program to address the mismatch between the large scale of the federal government and the very local level at which land-use decisions are usually made?

In appendix 2, we provide detailed responses to each of these problems; we only sketch them here. To solve the funding problem, we propose reducing the cap on the home mortgage interest deduction in high-price, low-construction counties from $1,000,000 to $300,000. While this is discussed at length below, the key point for now is that this reduction provides a funding source that can be used to encourage new development. That is, the added federal tax revenues generated once some owners in a given local area cannot deduct interest payments will be available to that area in the form of increased local aid if the county increases its level of new construction. If new construction rises enough, then the area can leave the program altogether (i.e., the cap returns to $1 million).

To solve the problem of which areas should participate, we propose that inclusion in the program be determined on a county-by-county basis. Good data are available at the county level, and counties are a reasonable proxy for housing markets. In some states, like Maryland, county governments even make land-use decisions. House price and permitting data determine whether the county qualifies for inclusion in the program.

Implementing our reforms requires that we can readily distinguish whether market areas have more or less flexible (elastic) or inflexible (inelastic) housing supplies. Hence, in appendix 2, we show how to separate each county in the United States into one of four types of markets: (a) those with high prices and relatively little construction, which have inflexible (inelastic) supply sides to their housing markets; (b) those with high levels of construction, but not high prices, which are flexible (elastic) in nature; (c) those with low prices and little construction, which is due to low levels of demand; and (d) those counties that do not fall into any of the other three categories.

More specifically, we use data from the 2000 census on 307 large counties that contain over 60 percent of the nation's population to simulate our proposed policy reform. Thirty-six counties, or about 12 percent, are classified as having very inflexible or inelastic supply sides to their housing markets, along with very high house prices. Thus, latent demand for these markets is very strong even though relatively little new housing is being built in them. Table A2-2 lists each county. Not surprisingly, counties along California's coastline and Amtrak's Northeast Corridor route from Washington, DC, to Boston dominate this list, along with a few other markets such as Honolulu. The average house price in these counties is nearly $400,000 in current dollars, so these areas are expensive by national standards. Their total number of annual housing permits is less than 1 percent of the local housing stock, so very little is being added to the stock in the face of high prices in these places.

It is noteworthy that nearly three times as many counties (101 to be exact) are classified as having very high levels of housing construction and modest price levels. Prices are not appreciably above construction costs in these places, so they have no fundamental affordability problem, and there is no reason for the government to push for more supply in them. Table A2-3 lists each of these counties with high numbers of housing permits and modest house prices.[8] Prices are much lower in these areas, averaging under $170,000 in today's dollars, or less than half the average in the inelastic group. Naturally, permitting activity is much higher, with the lowest rate for any county in this group adding at least 2 percent to its housing stock each year. Many of these counties are issuing permits that will increase their housing stocks by 3–4 percent per annum.

To solve the third problem, how to reconcile federal involvement in and local control over land-use regulations, we propose that this program be administered at the state level. Specifically, states will offer programs that are designed to increase the amount of new construction in their high-cost counties. The funds raised from changing the home mortgage interest deduction will be made available to the state's program if that program meets several clear criteria. The funds will continue flowing to the state's program only if there is a measurable increase in new construction in the state's high-cost counties.

One vital criterion for any program is that it must provide money only for government services (which include tax reductions) and only in the counties with owners who paid higher taxes due to the tighter mortgage cap. In other words, if $1 million is raised by lowering the mortgage cap in Montgomery County, MD, then $1 million must be allocated to different areas within Montgomery County, and not to other counties within the state or to other nongovernmental recipients. The program cannot directly subsidize developers or build housing. Second, the program must direct funding as a function of the number of housing permits issued. The federal government will ensure that the program actually has an effect by tying payouts from the state to new production in the county. By tying the funding to actual results, there is less need for Washington to micromanage the state plans. Because states have the incentive to design an effective funds allocation plan to avoid a funding cut-off, they and not Washington should operate these programs.

We recognize that this system could become very complicated with fifty different state programs. Fortunately, the high-cost, low-supply counties are in only eight states. Moreover, three of these states (Connecticut, Hawaii, and Maryland) have only one high-cost, low-supply county. Virginia has only two such counties. In fact, the only states that have a widespread problem with high costs and low development are California, Massachusetts, New Jersey, and New York. Thus, there really are only four states that will need to develop extensive programs to tie local aid to new development, although that certainly could change over time.

For these programs to really change the regulatory environment, communities must face strong incentives to build—at least $30,000 per unit. While this might seem like a prohibitively large amount of money, the next section shows that it is feasible to raise substantial sums by changing the home mortgage interest deduction in those areas with high prices and low levels of construction.[9] In some ways, this $30,000 figure may not seem much less than the $50,000 subsidy per unit under the LIHTC. However, that simple comparison is misleading because the $50,000 subsidy to LIHTC unit production represents either a real social cost (i.e., compensation for real expenses) or a transfer to developers. The $30,000 subsidy goes to local governments for them to use on public services like schools or safety or roads that internalize the negative externalities of development. This is not primarily a transfer program. If more production is generated, failures in the housing market are reduced and, hopefully, completely corrected.

Reforming the Home Mortgage Interest Deduction

We recommend reducing the maximum amount of mortgage debt on which interest can be deducted to $300,000, because we calculate that this will generate enough revenues to pay for a very generous subsidy program in the high-cost, low-supply states. In appendix 2 we calculate quantities based on a universal reduction in the maximum amount of deductible interest, but we also see a reasonable case for phasing in the change. For example, it might make sense to allow a much higher degree of deductibility on current mortgages, and to implement the new cap only on new mortgages or mortgages associated with new purchases. The phase-in of the cap could also take place over time for existing mortgages. These timing considerations are potentially important, but we will not focus on them here.

More generally, we note that keeping the mortgage interest deduction for moderate-sized mortgages ensures that the costs of this policy change will be borne almost entirely by the wealthiest Americans. Any tinkering regarding the phase-in of the mortgage interest deduction will be relevant primarily for people who are quite well-to-do.

While $300,000 is a reasonable cap that generates significant increases in tax revenues, it is certainly not the only plausible number. Higher caps will do a better job of making sure that middle-income people are not affected directly by this change in policy. Lower caps will raise more revenue. We believe that $300,000 balances these two competing goods, but acknowledge that a case can also be made for other figures.

How big an impact will this policy have on new supply and housing prices? We believe that a realistic estimate is that a $30,000 per-unit subsidy could increase new construction levels by 20 percent in many communities. Of course, our program would increase construction in only a modest number of communities, but that is precisely the point. America doesn't need a nationwide increase in building, but rather an increase in building in areas with high prices and little supply.

A 20 percent increase in annual construction levels would have only a modest impact on prices in the short run. After all, the overall price of housing is determined by the stock of existing homes, and in the areas that have restricted new building, construction levels are quite small relative to this stock. Over time, however, the increase in new building could increase the stock by 10 to 20 percent, which, given conventional elasticity estimates, could reduce prices by about the same amount. More importantly, by pushing against the tendency of local governments to reduce building, the program could stop localities from becoming even more restrictive and making the problem even worse.

Ensuring the Poor Can Consume Some Minimum Housing Quality: Vouchers

These changes will make housing more affordable in high-cost areas of the country for both middle-income and low-income Americans, but most of the poor will still face housing costs that are far above their ability to pay. For this reason, even if our policy to increase housing supply was successfully adopted, there would still be a need to make some minimum quality of housing accessible to the poorest Americans.

There are several characteristics of a good policy to increase housing affordability for the poor. It should be well targeted so that benefits go directly to the poor. It should be cheap to administer. It should not create perverse incentives to build in low-demand areas or to keep the poor fixed in communities that are lacking in economic opportunities. The LIHTC fails these tests because it is expensive, promotes new construction in places where building is unnecessary, and benefits developers as much as, or even more than, poorer residents. It should be eliminated, and the savings used for other programs or rebated to taxpayers.

An enlarged voucher program would do far more good than the LIHTC. In an ideal world, we would deal with the inability of poor people to afford housing by making poor people richer. If this is impossible, then housing vouchers—a direct transfer that is relatively easy to administer—are the best means of providing housing aid for the poorest Americans.

We do not know what the "right" amount of housing is for the poor. We have our own opinions as private citizens, which involve much generosity when children are involved and less when they are not, but these private opinions are not ultimately the province of economics. The decision on a minimum housing quality to be enjoyed by any citizen is properly determined by the values of our whole society. What economics can tell us, however, is that whatever the desired level of housing for the poor is, vouchers are the best way of achieving it. America has tried many different housing policies to improve housing for the least fortunate, and none has been nearly as effective as vouchers. Many of those policies, including rent control and some public housing projects, almost certainly have made things worse.

The Section 8 program has many attractive features, but it is not perfect. While vouchers in general are relatively cost-effective, tenant-based vouchers are preferable to project-based vouchers. One of the great virtues of vouchers is that they give as much choice as possible to their recipients, and this choice helps to ensure that the voucher's benefits go to the recipient. Project-based vouchers lack this virtue and are much more likely to benefit the project owner rather than the tenant.

Hence, we recommend that project-based vouchers be phased out, along with all other direct federal aid to developers. Project-based vouchers are meant to help subsidize new construction, and they suffer many of the same defects as the tax credit program. In low-cost areas where demand is low, such subsidies make little sense. There is no sound rationale for subsidizing building in areas where economic conditions do not support higher housing prices. In areas with highly elastic housing supply, we oppose project-based vouchers because these areas already have high levels of supply. Tenant-based vouchers, in contrast, will give their recipients a greater ability to move across space in response to economic opportunity.

Only in areas where supply is inelastic and prices are high do project-based vouchers make any sense at all. Yet we oppose them even in these areas and believe it makes more sense to convert all project-based vouchers into tenant-based vouchers. Not only are project-based vouchers a fairly inefficient means of encouraging new supply, but there is much to be gained by a single, simple national program.

While we have argued strongly against a one-size-fits-all rule in designing our supply-side policy and with respect to the home mortgage interest deduction, there is much more to be said for a nationwide policy for housing vouchers, which in effect constitutes an antipoverty program. After all, the point of these vouchers is not to fix failures in a few among many housing markets, but to give poor people everywhere more resources. Programs aimed at market failures need to target specific markets, but redistribution efforts such as the voucher program should be national in scope to reduce the tendency of redistribution to create poverty clusters. The recipients should be free to use those vouchers in any way that they want. In particular, they should be free to move across areas. A single voucher policy consisting only of tenant-based vouchers will make that mobility easier.

Currently, it can be hard for voucher recipients to move across metropolitan areas. Tenant-based vouchers are, in principle, portable. The ability of people to choose their areas of residence has been a major objective of the voucher program for several years. Still, there are regular complaints about the difficulties of moving the vouchers from one market area to another. The administration of vouchers at the housing authority level means that moving from one area to another requires the approval of two authorities. This may discourage some poorer households from moving to a stronger labor market where their long-run prospects might be better.

While it is possible to imagine modest increases in portability within the current system, some mobility will always be compromised if vouchers are administered by different local housing authorities. We recommend that vouchers be made portable nationwide and the program simplified administratively. The choices vouchers offer to recipients should not be compromised by limited portability.

Indeed, the voucher program seems sufficiently modest in size and sufficiently simple in operation that it could easily be run by a single national housing authority. This would remove local housing authorities from the allocation process. The voucher program should be turned into a transaction between the federal government and poor households that meet some clearly defined means test, without a local housing authority serving as a middleman. Note that this is not a call to turn the Section 8 program into a mandate, only to simplify the allocation system and to ensure that the mobility of the poor is not reduced by this program.

One objection to centralizing authority over the housing voucher program is that doing so makes it harder to monitor the quality of housing units within the program. We are not very concerned about this objection, because we suspect the current Section 8 standards in this regard are too high, not too low. While we certainly do not want people living in truly dilapidated units (without running water and functioning plumbing), such units now constitute a very small fraction of the housing stock. In fact, we would encourage some experimentation with lower-quality accommodations for some households (e.g., SRO-type units for singles) to see whether allowing occupancy of cheaper, lower-quality housing leads to more housing for more of the poor. In any case, the real judge of unit quality should be the consumer, not some well-intentioned program official.

Summary and Conclusion

The current drop in housing prices should not lead us to forget that prices in many American markets remain quite high, both relative to historical standards and relative to construction costs. Increased supply in markets where house prices are well above physical production costs should be the primary focus of a new national housing policy that is not targeted exclusively at the poor. Most importantly, we recommend changing the home mortgage interest deduction to help fund such a program. More specifically, we propose implementing a new, lower cap on the amount of mortgage debt on which interest can be deducted. Our proposal is for a $300,000 cap, which would affect just over 4 percent of owner-occupied households. The cap would then be waived for borrowers in all markets except those with inelastic housing supplies. The additional taxes that the federal government would collect from large mortgage borrowers in these inelastically supplied markets would then be rebated to the local governments who permit new housing construction.

While we appreciate the ability of supply-side subsidy programs to address the key underlying issue affecting affordability in our most expensive markets—namely, inefficiently low housing production—we are not favorably disposed to the LIHTC program. This program is very costly to administer, and its design is such that many of its benefits are captured by developers, not poorer households in particular. The fact that there is a long queue of developers applying for credits—roughly three times the amount of credits are being sought as are available—is a clear signal that the program is providing very high risk-adjusted returns for builders. Hence, we recommend the elimination of the LIHTC program.

Finally, the affordability problem of the truly poor should be met with a simplified voucher program, if society deems that direct cash transfers are not preferable. Vouchers should be fully portable across all housing markets and administered by a single national authority, eliminating local housing authorities as middlemen in this process.

Appendix 1
Economic Incidence Analysis
of a Subsidy

This appendix elaborates on and supports the economic incidence analyses discussed earlier. We look here at per-unit subsidies to demand, limited subsidies to demand, and supply-side subsidies.

Per-Unit Subsidies to Demand

Any program that offers a per-unit subsidy for demanders has the impact depicted in figure A1-1. This graph illustrates the classic analysis of a demand-side subsidy with three different supply curves. The impact of a general demand subsidy is to shift the demand curve out from D to D^1 and create a wedge between the price that suppliers receive and the price that consumers pay. The amount of the wedge is the degree of the subsidy. As we have discussed in previous chapters, the impact of this shift in the demand curve depends on the shape of the supply curve.

Supply Curve A—the upward sloping supply curve—displays a moderate degree of elasticity or flexibility in terms of new housing supply. The impact of subsidizing demand in this case is to increase both the quantity and price of housing. In this case, both consumers and suppliers benefit from the subsidy.

Supply Curve B—the flat supply curve—is a completely elastic supply curve. Houston is perhaps the market most closely approximated by these supply conditions. More than sixty thousand new units were supplied in 2005 and more than seventy thousand units were supplied in 2007,

FIGURE A1-1

DEMAND SUBSIDIES AND THE ELASTICITY OF SUPPLY

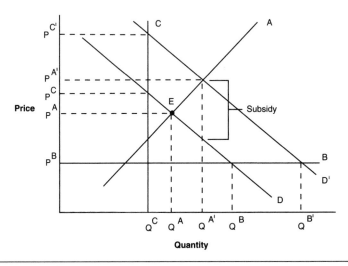

SOURCE: Authors' illustration.

despite the fact that housing prices are quite moderate in Harris County, Texas. Note that the demand subsidy causes quantity to rise, but not price. In this case, consumers, not suppliers, reap all of the benefits from a demand subsidy. If demand subsidies are meant to increase the consumption of housing and to benefit consumers while doing so, this represents the best-case scenario.

Supply Curve C—the vertical supply curve—is a completely inelastic supply curve. This curve is an extreme version of conditions in certain suburban markets where land-use regulations have virtually stopped the production of new housing, or in declining areas where new production of housing has come to a halt because prices (both before and after the subsidy) remain below the cost of new construction. When supply is completely inelastic, the subsidy-induced shift in demand causes prices to rise but brings about no change in housing consumed. All of the benefits in this case accrue to the suppliers and none to the consumers. This represents the worst case for a demand-side subsidy, since there is no benefit for the consumer and no change in overall housing consumption.

Figure A1-2
Partial Demand Subsidies

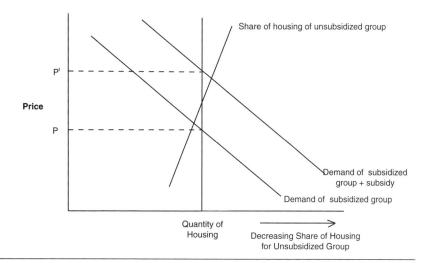

Share of housing of unsubsidized group

P'

Price

P

Demand of subsidized group + subsidy

Demand of subsidized group

Quantity of Housing

Decreasing Share of Housing for Unsubsidized Group

Source: Authors' illustration.

Limited Subsidies to Demand

Figure A1-2 analyzes the impact of a limited subsidy in markets with fixed supply. In this case, the horizontal axis reflects the share of housing consumed by the group that receives the subsidy, not the total amount of housing consumed. The downward sloping demand curve reflects the demand by that subsidized group. The upward sloping curve reflects the share of housing consumed by the group that does not receive the subsidy. Points to the right of the intersection are where this group consumes less, so the upward slope of that curve reflects the fact that this group consumes less as the price rises. Just as in figure A1-1, the subsidy shifts out the demand curve by creating a wedge between the price that the subsidized group pays and the price that suppliers receive for providing their homes. The impact of this shift is a rise in prices and an increased share of housing being consumed by the subsidized group.

In this case, suppliers are not the only people who benefit from the demand subsidy. The subsidized group also benefits, although this group's benefits will be less than the overall costs of the subsidy, since the benefits are shared with suppliers. The nonsubsidized group is made worse off by the subsidy, since it faces higher prices with no offsetting subsidy. If the demand curves are linear and have exactly the same slope, then the price paid by the nonsubsidized group will rise by exactly one-half of the subsidy. We should also expect to see a shift in housing consumption between the two groups.

Supply-Side Subsidies

Classic supply-side subsidies are thought to have the same effects as demand-side subsidies, but this is not the case in the housing market, as we have indicated. In a standard analysis, supply-side policies represent a subsidy to sellers, and this will result in reduced prices and increased quantity. If each seller receives a bonus from the government for selling the product, then in perfectly elastic areas, the price falls by exactly the amount of the subsidy. In inelastic areas, the sellers pocket the subsidy and there is no change in quantity or price to the buyer. In areas with moderately elastic levels of supply, the policy affects both quantity and price. An important prediction of economic theory at its most basic is that supply-side subsidies and demand-side subsidies have identical incidence on both buyers and sellers.

However, this classic analysis does not pertain to the housing market because supply-side subsidies are not subsidies to sellers, but subsidies to builders. A typical supply-side subsidy program such as the LIHTC ensures that a small number of builders receive a federal bonus for building new homes. However, most sellers of housing are existing homeowners who do not directly receive any subsidy, and in areas with large construction sectors, most builders also receive no subsidy. Consequently, we must consider the impact of a supply-side subsidy by looking at what effect subsidizing a limited number of units will have on the overall price and quantity of housing.

The key question is whether subsidies to new construction crowd out other building. We discussed this issue in a previous chapter and noted the evidence suggesting that this crowd-out is heterogeneous across areas. This is quite compatible with the predictions of standard economic theory. If the supply of nonsubsidized new construction is perfectly elastic and if there is plenty of nonsubsidized new construction, then the impact of subsidized construction will be a perfect crowd-out of nonsubsidized construction. For this reason, subsidizing new units in highly elastic markets will have no impact on the aggregate number of housing units being produced and no impact on price. Thus, there are extensive program costs but no impact on overall affordability conditions.

However, if the supply of nonsubsidized new construction is perfectly inelastic, then any new units created by subsidization will add one for one to the housing stock. In this case, subsidization will create a shift outward in the supply curve, which will increase quantity and decrease prices. When nonsubsidized construction is inelastic, suppliers will benefit from this subsidy, but so will consumers through lower prices. This result suggests that subsidizing housing in inelastic regions can have desirable effects, while subsidizing housing in regions with elastic housing supply makes little sense.

Appendix 2
Implementation of Our
Proposed Policy Reform

This appendix provides the underlying analytical details to our proposed policy reform. Specifically, it explains how the program would determine which housing markets were covered under it—which markets, that is, were suffering from a market failure in the sense that supply is too limited. It also explains how the program would be funded and administered. We certainly do not view our analysis as definitive, but rather as the starting point for the design of a new and much more effective affordability policy. At the very least, the analysis confirms that it is feasible to design a reasonable policy with available data and resources.

Summary of Our Reform Proposal

(1) Make the Section 8 voucher program central to dealing with the poor's affordability problems, and reform that program as follows:

    a. Convert all project-based vouchers to tenant-based vouchers.

    b. Make all vouchers completely portable across the country to encourage the mobility of poorer households.

    c. Reduce administrative complexity by eliminating the role of local housing authorities in allocating the vouchers.

    d. Now that the low end of the housing quality distribution includes so few dilapidated, substandard units, experiment with relaxing the unit quality standards for program participation.

(2) Eliminate the Low Income Housing Tax Credit subsidized production program.

    a. This program is inferior to vouchers in dealing with the poor's affordability problem because it does not directly transfer resources to them.

    b. It is wasteful in the sense that many subsidized units are built in markets with very flexible supplies, so that these units simply crowd out those that would have been delivered by the market anyway. Because the credits are allocated by state population and are not sensitive to conditions of specific markets, the program also ends up subsidizing construction in declining markets, where there is no good reason for the government to be providing more housing.

    c. It is also wasteful in the sense that the program functions so that developers reap most of the benefits no matter where the units are built. The huge excess demand by developers to participate in the program speaks volumes about this point.

    d. The program does generate some production of housing units in markets with inflexible or inelastic supply sides, but there are better ways to encourage such building. It is to that issue that our proposal now turns.

(3) Cap the deduction of mortgage interest at the first $300,000 of debt. Then lift the cap for all homeowners living in counties that do not have inelastic supplies of housing and high prices (i.e., everywhere but the thirty-six counties listed in appendix table A2-2). Next, have the federal government rebate the tax savings back to the local areas in exchange for sustained increases in housing unit construction. Finally, lift the cap on the mortgage interest deduction if the inelastically supplied counties show sufficient long-term increases in housing unit production.

    a. Fewer than one in twenty owners has mortgage debt that would be subject to this cap. However, those households do live disproportionately in the markets with both high house prices and low levels of housing construction.

b. Substantial enough revenues would be raised that permitting rates would likely more than double in some counties, even assuming that it takes $30,000 to induce a highly regulated locality to allow one new building permit.

c. Our policy targets high-income, high-tax-bracket households with more than $300,000 in mortgage debt neither out of animus toward the rich nor out of concern for general equity. Rather, it does so because the mortgage interest deduction functions primarily to drive up house prices in places that tightly regulate development (see figure 5-1). Because the mortgage interest and local property tax deductions do not improve affordability even for those residing in these inelastically supplied markets who itemize on their tax returns, and because they make things worse for everyone else who does not itemize, making the cap increasingly binding is a good idea in and of itself.[1]

d. An attractive feature of this reform is that it provides incentives for localities to increase the supply of housing and rewards them (and their high-income taxpayers) for sustained increases in housing production. At the very least, it encourages those residents subject to the cap to favor, rather than oppose, new housing construction because more housing is the only way to get the cap lifted. It is important to recognize that local governments do not impose restrictions on residential development simply out of spite. Rather, they are responding to the desires of their residents, who perceive costs associated with growth. The goal here is to provide localities with additional resources to compensate their residents for the downside to growth. This motivation is what differentiates our proposal from that of President Bush's Advisory Panel on Federal Tax Reform. That panel advocated that more, not less, mortgage interest be deductible in more expensive areas. We recognize the concerns that led to this conclusion, but believe that efficiency concerns push in exactly the opposite direction. We propose that the savings to the federal government be used in a way that encourages more housing precisely in the markets with true affordability problems—that is, in markets where prices are far higher than production costs.

Defining Elastic and Inelastic Regions of the Country

To reform housing policy in a way that differentiates between more and less elastic regions of the country obviously requires a sensible way to categorize markets. Our strategy for assessing the degree of housing supply inelasticity is based on both price and new construction. This methodology will help us in assessing the regions that will be affected by our proposed reforms, and the methodology is itself a part of our policy proposal since it suggests regional differences in policies will hinge critically on how regions are defined.

Our approach is to treat counties as distinct housing markets. Using the U.S. Census of Population and Housing, it is possible to obtain housing price data for tracts, cities, counties, metropolitan areas, and states. Using the Census of Construction, it is possible to amass construction statistics for states, metropolitan areas, counties, and cities, but not for smaller geographic areas. This latter fact means that subcity areas such as neighborhoods cannot be used as housing markets.

In many ways, it would be desirable to have the federal government deal directly with states rather than with a lower level of government, since there is so much precedent for federal-state interactions. However, in larger states such as New York and California, the heterogeneity in housing supply conditions is extreme. Given that California contains inland areas with extremely elastic supply and coastal areas with extremely inelastic supply, we cannot see the benefit of moving from a nationwide policy to a California-wide policy. In addition to California and New York, states with wildly different housing conditions within their borders include Massachusetts, New Jersey, Virginia, Florida, Washington, and Oregon. In sum, states are just too big to meaningfully use as housing markets.

Localities also are problematic to use as housing markets because they are so heterogeneous and often too small to effectively connect with the federal government. In addition, much of the country is in unincorporated areas. That leaves two plausible candidates for meaningful housing market areas: metropolitan areas and counties. Metropolitan areas are, of course, made up of counties, so in a sense the distinction between these two choices is modest. We prefer counties because the entire United States is in some county jurisdiction but not in a metropolitan area. In addition, counties are smaller and can capture some of the heterogeneity within an urban area.

Metropolitan areas are also frequently redefined by the census, which would confuse matters, while counties are not.

Three pieces of information about each county can be used to quantify its housing market situation: housing prices, construction levels, and the size of the existing housing stock. Of these, construction levels are the most readily available. Housing permits are available for each county on an annual basis from the Construction Statistics section of the U.S Commerce Department web site. Permits do not precisely equal units put in place, but they are an excellent proxy for the amount of new housing supply that a local area is willing to allow.

Housing stock and price are available at decadal frequencies from the U.S. Census of Population and Housing. The stock is an excellent assessment of the size of the housing market in the census year, and it can be updated using permit data combined with estimates of the depreciation of the housing stock. In most cases, the housing stock moves sufficiently slowly that the updating procedure is fairly irrelevant to the overall number. House prices are self-reported in the decennial census, and while that introduces measurement error, its nature is well understood, and these data remain a reliable indicator of demand in the sense that high prices in a market invariably reflect strong demand, at least in part.[2]

The stock of housing is measured by the number of units reported in the decennial census. The supply of new units is captured by the total number of permits issued within a county from 2000 through 2006. Table A2-1 lists the ten counties that issued the most permits and the ten counties that issued the fewest; these are drawn from a group of large counties that constituted the top 10 percent nationwide in terms of housing units as of 2000.[3] We also report the share of permits issued in each county over the past seven years (2000–2006) as a fraction of its existing housing stock in 2000. Because so many U.S. counties are nearly empty of people and homes, we focus on this group of large counties in our analysis; the 182.7 million people who live in these 307 counties represent the bulk of the nation's population. Moreover, this focus allows us not to worry about misleadingly large permit shares of existing stock that can (and do) result from even small permit issuances in tiny rural housing markets.

The extraordinary heterogeneity in permitting activity, even within the group of large counties, is evident in this table. The ten lowest permit

TABLE A2-1
PERMIT ISSUANCE IN LARGE U.S. COUNTIES
Top and Bottom 10 Counties of the 307 Largest
U.S. Counties by Housing Stock

	Top 10 counties by permit issuance 2000–2006	
County name	Permits issued, 2000–2006	Permits issued as fraction of stock
Maricopa County, Arizona	318,453	0.25
Harris County, Texas	250,662	0.19
Clark County, Nevada	231,179	0.41
Riverside County, California	179,229	0.31
Los Angeles County, California	147,848	0.05
Miami-Dade County, Florida	125,603	0.15
Lee County, Florida	115,371	0.47
Tarrant County, Texas	110,661	0.20
Cook County, Illinois	108,675	0.05
San Diego County, California	101,796	0.10

	Bottom 10 counties by permit issuance 2000–2006	
County name	Permits issued, 2000–2006	Permits issued as fraction of stock
St. Louis city, Missouri	3,847	0.02
Niagara County, New York	3,817	0.04
Rockland County, New York	3,677	0.04
Lackawanna County, Pennsylvania	3,517	0.04
Richmond city, Virginia	3,445	0.04
Trumbull County, Ohio	3,133	0.03
Beaver County, Pennsylvania	2,949	0.04
Oneida County, New York	2,461	0.02
Broome County, New York	1,576	0.02
Kanawha County, West Virginia	1,549	0.02

SOURCES: U.S. Census Bureau Manufacturing, Mining and Construction Statistics. County Building Permits 2000–2004. Washington, D.C.: U.S. Census Bureau, 2000–2006; U.S. Census Bureau. 2000 Decennial Census, County Housing Characteristics. Washington, D.C.: U.S. Census Bureau, 2000.

FIGURE A2-1

PERMITS AND MEDIAN HOUSE PRICES IN LARGE COUNTIES

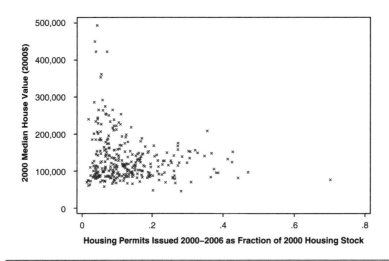

Housing Permits Issued 2000–2006 as Fraction of 2000 Housing Stock

SOURCES: U.S. Census Bureau Manufacturing, Mining and Construction Statistics. County Building Permits 2000–2004. Washington, D.C.: U.S. Census Bureau, 2000–2006; U.S. Census Bureau. 2000 Decennial Census, County Housing Characteristics. Washington, D.C.: U.S. Census Bureau, 2000.

issuance levels among these large counties over the past seven years are quite low, ranging from 1,549 to 3,847. Shares of beginning-of-period stock also are low, ranging from 1.7 to 4.0 percent. The top ten issuers each approved at least one hundred thousand permits over the same time period. Harris County, TX (Houston), and Maricopa County, AZ (Phoenix), each issued at least a quarter of a million permits. There is wide variation in how big a gross addition to the local housing stock these permits represent. For Lee County, FL (Fort Myers), and Clark County, NV (Las Vegas), permits issued between 2000 and 2006 are over 40 percent of the 2000 stock. However, large absolute permit levels in Cook County, IL (Chicago), and Los Angeles County, CA, are only 5 percent of their beginning-of-period stocks.[4]

We use the ratio of permits issued between 2000 and 2006 divided by the housing stock in 2000 as our basis measure of supply conditions in the county. Figure A2-1 graphs the relationship between prices in the year 2000 and this ratio for the group of 307 large counties discussed above. The graph visually depicts the fact discussed in a previous chapter—namely, that counties with abundant new construction are not expensive and counties that are expensive do not have abundant new construction.[5] In addition, the cluster of observations around the origin of this figure indicates that many counties do not have high average house price or high permitting levels, which is an indicator of low demand.

We next divide American counties into four groups. The first three conform to the categories discussed above: (a) places with high house prices and low permitting intensity; these are counties with inelastic supplies of housing; (b) places with high permitting intensity and moderate house prices; these have elastic supplies of housing; and (c) low-demand counties; these places have inelastic supply sides to their housing markets, but need to be treated differently for the purposes of policy analysis because they suffer from low demand, in contrast to the high demand facing the inelastic markets in the first group. The fourth group is comprised of counties that are not easily placed in one of the other three types of housing markets.

Cities in the first group must have mean house prices above $230,000 (in 2000 dollars) and permit share figures below 0.1 (10 percent).[6] The average house value across all 307 counties in our sample was $162,720. We chose the $230,000 price cutoff because it is well above the sample mean, so we can be sure that prices are more than enough above physical construction costs to justify substantial new construction.[7] However, this group of counties does not permit intensely, as the 0.10 cutoff for the permit share variable is well below the 0.13 mean for the 307 counties in this sample.

The average population of the thirty-six counties in this group that we classify as having inelastic supplies is just over one million, and they contain over 425,000 housing units on average. In aggregate, forty-one million people live in over fifteen million housing units in these counties. The average house price in this subsample is $322,040 in 2000 dollars and about $375,000 in 2006 dollars. The full range runs from $232,522 to $585,462 in 2000 dollars, and from $272,214 to $685,400 in current dollars.[8] The average permit share of the 2000 housing stock is 5.9 percent, indicating that total permits average less than 1 percent of the stock annually in these very high-priced markets. These counties with high prices yet relatively low permitting intensity exhibit both high demand and inelastic supply. In the absence of binding regulatory barriers, we would expect much more construction in them.

TABLE A2-2

LARGE COUNTIES WITH INELASTIC HOUSING SUPPLY

County name	Mean house value (2000$)	Permits share
Alameda County, California	$338,237	5.8%
Los Angeles County, California	$276,483	4.5%
Marin County, California	$585,462	4.3%
Monterey County, California	$336,890	6.7%
Orange County, California	$305,693	6.9%
San Diego County, California	$264,983	9.8%
San Francisco County, California	$505,891	3.9%
San Mateo County, California	$539,066	3.6%
Santa Barbara County, California	$365,470	5.9%
Santa Clara County, California	$498,550	7.1%
Santa Cruz County, California	$397,317	5.3%
Sonoma County, California	$315,808	8.7%
Ventura County, California	$281,612	9.1%
Fairfield County, Connecticut	$368,178	4.7%
District of Columbia	$240,863	4.2%
Honolulu County, Hawaii	$309,745	6.6%
Montgomery County, Maryland	$269,156	9.0%
Barnstable County, Massachusetts	$232,522	6.7%
Essex County, Massachusetts	$249,962	5.3%
Middlesex County, Massachusetts	$296,419	4.5%
Norfolk County, Massachusetts	$286,638	5.4%
Suffolk County, Massachusetts	$254,335	3.4%
Bergen County, New Jersey	$299,223	4.4%
Essex County, New Jersey	$244,199	5.2%
Monmouth County, New Jersey	$246,470	7.6%
Morris County, New Jersey	$303,317	7.6%
Somerset County, New Jersey	$284,310	9.1%
Union County, New Jersey	$233,373	3.9%
Kings County, New York	$270,737	4.5%
Nassau County, New York	$301,653	1.9%

continued on next page

Table A2-2 continued

County name	Mean house value (2000$)	Permits share
New York County, New York	$496,684	5.5%
Richmond County, New York	$244,843	8.7%
Rockland County, New York	$259,030	3.9%
Westchester County, New York	$361,785	3.4%
Arlington County, Virginia	$265,052	8.0%
Fairfax County, Virginia	$264,901	9.8%

SOURCES: U.S. Census Bureau Manufacturing, Mining and Construction Statistics. County Building Permits 2000–2004. Washington, D.C.: U.S. Census Bureau, 2000–2006; U.S. Census Bureau. 2000 Decennial Census, County Housing Characteristics. Washington, D.C.: U.S. Census Bureau, 2000.
NOTES: House values are from the 2000 U.S. census in 2000$. Permits share is the ratio of all housing permits issued 2000–2006 to the aggregate housing stock as of the year 2000.

Table A2-2 lists each of the thirty-six high-demand counties that issue few permits, along with their mean house values and permit share numbers. Not surprisingly, this list of inelastic markets is dominated by counties all along the coast of California and Amtrak's Northeast Corridor from Washington, DC, to Boston, with a few other markets such as Honolulu County, HI.

Table A2-3 provides the analogous information for the places with high permitting rates that also have high demand and appear to satisfy it by building more and more housing units. There is a single cutoff for this group with elastic supplies of housing—namely, to be in the top one-third of all large counties in terms of permitting intensity. Each of the 101 counties in this group has issued permits between 2000 and 2006 equal to at least 14.4 percent of their housing stock as of 2000. Thus, for these seven years, each county in this group issued permits in amounts equal to at least 2 percent of its total housing stock (on average). This group is dominated by high-growth Sunbelt markets running from North Carolina to Florida, and then west to the California border. There are a few other interior markets in this group, too. These counties definitely are doing their part to build the housing that America's growing population needs.

Average house price for this group of counties is only $143,899 in 2000 dollars and is still under $170,000 in current dollars. These values are well

TABLE A2-3
LARGE COUNTIES WITH ELASTIC HOUSING SUPPLY

County name	Mean house value (2000$)	Permits share
Baldwin County, Alabama	$141,853	37.5%
Maricopa County, Arizona	$155,731	25.5%
Mohave County, Arizona	$95,265	26.4%
Pima County, Arizona	$131,218	16.6%
Pinal County, Arizona	$95,866	70.2%
Yavapai County, Arizona	$146,522	27.3%
Kern County, California	$106,481	17.1%
Placer County, California	$251,154	35.6%
Riverside County, California	$159,722	30.7%
Sacramento County, California	$164,471	15.4%
San Joaquin County, California	$164,261	20.7%
Stanislaus County, California	$149,771	16.7%
Adams County, Colorado	$150,729	26.1%
Arapahoe County, Colorado	$209,596	18.1%
El Paso County, Colorado	$171,230	21.3%
Larimer County, Colorado	$197,824	20.5%
Sussex County, Delaware	$132,993	21.5%
Alachua County, Florida	$112,676	14.8%
Bay County, Florida	$106,491	25.8%
Brevard County, Florida	$109,815	20.2%
Charlotte County, Florida	$114,555	26.3%
Collier County, Florida	$235,296	32.9%
Duval County, Florida	$111,427	18.9%
Hillsborough County, Florida	$119,943	21.9%
Lake County, Florida	$103,341	36.6%
Lee County, Florida	$135,627	47.0%
Leon County, Florida	$126,265	17.1%
Manatee County, Florida	$123,467	23.5%
Marion County, Florida	$90,896	31.1%
Miami-Dade County, Florida	$152,483	14.7%

continued on next page

Table A2-3 continued

County name	Mean house value (2000$)	Permits share
Okaloosa County, Florida	$126,899	18.9%
Orange County, Florida	$132,468	26.2%
Palm Beach County, Florida	$164,686	15.4%
Pasco County, Florida	$84,767	26.6%
Polk County, Florida	$85,352	23.8%
Sarasota County, Florida	$166,410	21.8%
Seminole County, Florida	$140,383	17.6%
St. Lucie County, Florida	$97,735	44.2%
Volusia County, Florida	$102,009	17.3%
Chatham County, Georgia	$133,905	14.5%
Clayton County, Georgia	$103,187	22.8%
Cobb County, Georgia	$174,193	17.4%
DeKalb County, Georgia	$169,624	16.6%
Fulton County, Georgia	$243,424	27.3%
Gwinnett County, Georgia	$162,547	34.8%
Ada County, Idaho	$149,189	29.9%
Kane County, Illinois	$190,689	27.3%
McHenry County, Illinois	$197,474	27.3%
Will County, Illinois	$176,529	30.8%
Polk County, Iowa	$118,832	17.4%
Johnson County, Kansas	$182,837	18.8%
Fayette County, Kentucky	$142,196	14.4%
St. Tammany Parish, Louisiana	$140,932	24.6%
Harford County, Maryland	$165,159	15.9%
Ottawa County, Michigan	$151,226	16.5%
Anoka County, Minnesota	$138,914	15.8%
Harrison County, Mississippi	$107,088	15.8%
Dakota County, Minnesota	$167,476	16.3%
Greene County, Missouri	$112,005	19.2%
St. Charles County, Missouri	$139,360	27.7%
Wake County, North Carolina	$187,242	32.2%
Bernalillo County, New Mexico	$142,965	15.4%

continued on next page

Table A2-3 continued

County name	Mean house value (2000$)	Permits share
Clark County, Nevada	$153,519	41.3%
Washoe County, Nevada	$188,683	24.2%
Buncombe County, North Carolina	$131,179	15.2%
Durham County, North Carolina	$152,273	21.6%
Forsyth County, North Carolina	$134,087	15.2%
Guilford County, North Carolina	$142,724	17.9%
Mecklenburg County, North Carolina	$183,508	28.5%
New Hanover County, North Carolina	$173,288	23.4%
Jackson County, Oregon	$161,334	16.0%
Washington County, Oregon	$208,151	16.8%
Charleston County, South Carolina	$179,324	22.9%
Greenville County, South Carolina	$131,325	16.0%
Horry County, South Carolina	$117,713	38.6%
Lexington County, South Carolina	$115,172	15.9%
Richland County, South Carolina	$127,187	19.3%
Bell County, Texas	$90,572	21.9%
Bexar County, Texas	$94,116	16.5%
Brazoria County, Texas	$95,263	25.8%
Cameron County, Texas	$64,499	20.3%
Collin County, Texas	$181,434	42.7%
Denton County, Texas	$154,338	23.1%
Fort Bend County, Texas	$137,678	19.6%
Galveston County, Texas	$105,210	18.6%
Harris County, Texas	$119,435	19.3%
Hidalgo County, Texas	$61,658	28.2%
Lubbock County, Texas	$81,718	14.5%
Montgomery County, Texas	$130,802	38.1%
Tarrant County, Texas	$115,332	19.6%
Travis County, Texas	$173,010	25.3%
Williamson County, Texas	$140,994	42.5%
Utah County, Utah	$183,987	30.4%
Chesterfield County, Virginia	$141,868	19.6%

continued on next page

Table A2-3 continued

County name	Mean house value (2000$)	Permits share
Prince William County, Virginia	$169,373	36.8%
Clark County, Washington	$181,440	19.0%
Pierce County, Washington	$167,851	14.4%
Snohomish County, Washington	$212,264	17.2%
Thurston County, Washington	$159,724	16.9%
Brown County, Wisconsin	$134,664	15.0%
Dane County, Wisconsin	$172,430	17.3%

SOURCES: U.S. Census Bureau Manufacturing, Mining and Construction Statistics. County Building Permits 2000–2004. Washington, D.C.: U.S. Census Bureau, 2000–2006; U.S. Census Bureau. 2000 Decennial Census, County Housing Characteristics. Washington, D.C.: U.S. Census Bureau, 2000.
NOTES: House values from the 2000 U.S. census in 2000$. Permits share is the ratio of all housing permits issued 2000–2006 to the aggregate housing stock as of the year 2000.

below the sample mean for the year 2000.[9] The average permitting share is 23.6 percent for this group, so permitting activity is indeed strong. The average population is nearly 508,000, and given the larger number of counties, the aggregate population living in these places is about 52 million. Thus, more people are living in elastic than in inelastic counties.

The low-demand counties are listed in table A2-4. The 118 counties in this group have both lower than average house prices (<$162,720 in the year 2000) and permit shares (<0.13). These counties represent a wide swath of places across the country. In particular, they include a high concentration of older, Rustbelt communities running all along the Great Lakes from Upstate New York through Michigan. Mean house price among these counties is only $118,869 in 2000 dollars ($139,160 in current dollars), and the average permit share is only 7.6 percent. These counties are no smaller than the elastic group in population terms, with the average county having 458,628 residents. In aggregate, 54.1 million people live in 22.9 million housing units in these counties that are in relative decline. While it may seem odd that such a large number of people live in such markets, we have shown in other work that it is the extreme durability of the housing stock that allows these places to endure in the face of relatively low demand (Glaeser and Gyourko 2005).

TABLE A2-4
LARGE COUNTIES WITH LOW DEMAND

County name	Mean house value (2000$)	Permits share
Jefferson County, Alabama	$122,170	8.7%
Mobile County, Alabama	$97,858	9.2%
Montgomery County, Alabama	$113,507	7.8%
Pulaski County, Arkansas	$108,483	8.3%
Butte County, California	$132,688	11.9%
New Castle County, Delaware	$154,721	7.3%
Broward County, Florida	$135,090	8.8%
Escambia County, Florida	$102,433	12.1%
Pinellas County, Florida	$115,720	4.7%
Muscogee County, Georgia	$104,268	10.1%
Richmond County, Georgia	$88,491	6.6%
Champaign County, Illinois	$107,214	12.6%
Madison County, Illinois	$93,049	9.1%
Peoria County, Illinois	$105,118	6.6%
Sangamon County, Illinois	$107,403	7.3%
St. Clair County, Illinois	$90,074	10.8%
Winnebago County, Illinois	$104,364	10.6%
Allen County, Indiana	$107,876	10.6%
Lake County, Indiana	$113,584	8.7%
Marion County, Indiana	$116,521	9.0%
St. Joseph County, Indiana	$105,002	7.6%
Vanderburgh County, Indiana	$101,666	8.0%
Sedgwick County, Kansas	$97,454	9.7%
Jefferson County, Kentucky	$130,020	7.6%
Caddo Parish, Louisiana	$88,594	5.2%
Calcasieu Parish, Louisiana	$86,709	8.9%
East Baton Rouge Parish, Louisiana	$124,076	10.3%
Jefferson Parish, Louisiana	$131,910	4.0%
Orleans Parish, Louisiana	$130,586	2.4%
Cumberland County, Maine	$159,456	9.6%
York County, Maine	$148,916	11.5%
Baltimore city, Maryland	$85,919	1.4%
Baltimore County, Maryland	$161,517	5.6%

continued on next page

Table A2-4 continued

County name	Mean house value (2000$)	Permits share
Prince George's County, Maryland	$155,731	6.8%
Hampden County, Massachusetts	$130,067	3.3%
Genesee County, Michigan	$106,750	8.5%
Ingham County, Michigan	$119,341	5.9%
Kalamazoo County, Michigan	$127,012	9.7%
Kent County, Michigan	$134,332	9.8%
Macomb County, Michigan	$149,063	10.4%
Saginaw County, Michigan	$97,884	5.0%
Wayne County, Michigan	$121,100	3.9%
Ramsey County, Minnesota	$142,272	5.2%
St. Louis County, Minnesota	$90,516	5.7%
Hinds County, Mississippi	$95,013	6.4%
Clay County, Missouri	$121,408	6.5%
St. Louis city, Missouri	$79,598	2.2%
St. Louis County, Missouri	$157,343	3.9%
Douglas County, Nebraska	$123,401	12.9%
Lancaster County, Nebraska	$125,653	12.9%
Hillsborough County, New Hampshire	$154,877	9.0%
Atlantic County, New Jersey	$137,845	11.9%
Burlington County, New Jersey	$158,186	9.2%
Camden County, New Jersey	$125,695	4.5%
Gloucester County, New Jersey	$131,726	12.5%
Ocean County, New Jersey	$147,710	10.4%
Albany County, New York	$131,041	4.3%
Broome County, New York	$85,429	1.8%
Erie County, New York	$102,834	3.4%
Monroe County, New York	$118,196	4.5%
Niagara County, New York	$90,033	4.0%
Oneida County, New York	$83,158	2.4%
Onondaga County, New York	$101,177	4.4%
Orange County, New York	$162,710	10.4%
Saratoga County, New York	$126,483	10.0%
Ulster County, New York	$133,019	6.6%
Gaston County, North Carolina	$102,110	11.4%
Cuyahoga County, Ohio	$137,038	2.3%

continued on next page

Table A2-4 continued

County name	Mean house value (2000$)	Permits share
Franklin County, Ohio	$138,024	12.3%
Hamilton County, Ohio	$147,788	3.7%
Lake County, Ohio	$145,540	6.5%
Lorain County, Ohio	$132,977	11.9%
Lucas County, Ohio	$109,877	5.2%
Mahoning County, Ohio	$94,274	3.8%
Montgomery County, Ohio	$115,087	4.4%
Stark County, Ohio	$118,225	5.9%
Summit County, Ohio	$133,185	6.7%
Trumbull County, Ohio	$97,962	3.3%
Cleveland County, Oklahoma	$102,056	12.5%
Oklahoma County, Oklahoma	$95,488	11.9%
Tulsa County, Oklahoma	$109,394	9.1%
Lane County, Oregon	$158,812	8.4%
Marion County, Oregon	$151,691	11.4%
Allegheny County, Pennsylvania	$106,194	3.1%
Beaver County, Pennsylvania	$94,000	3.8%
Berks County, Pennsylvania	$120,712	8.1%
Cumberland County, Pennsylvania	$133,433	9.7%
Dauphin County, Pennsylvania	$116,760	6.2%
Delaware County, Pennsylvania	$155,857	3.4%
Erie County, Pennsylvania	$99,610	4.5%
Lackawanna County, Pennsylvania	$111,248	3.7%
Lancaster County, Pennsylvania	$138,999	9.0%
Lehigh County, Pennsylvania	$133,457	8.1%
Luzerne County, Pennsylvania	$99,394	3.9%
Northampton County, Pennsylvania	$135,700	11.5%
Philadelphia County, Pennsylvania	$75,529	1.8%
Washington County, Pennsylvania	$108,732	7.0%
Westmoreland County, Pennsylvania	$106,607	4.6%
York County, Pennsylvania	$124,420	12.4%
Providence County, Rhode Island	$141,360	3.0%
Spartanburg County, South Carolina	$105,174	12.8%
Davidson County, Tennessee	$153,137	11.6%

continued on next page

Table A2-4 continued

County name	Mean house value (2000$)	Permits share
Hamilton County, Tennessee	$123,741	10.0%
Shelby County, Tennessee	$126,499	10.7%
Dallas County, Texas	$133,755	11.9%
El Paso County, Texas	$79,191	13.0%
Jefferson County, Texas	$72,716	6.3%
McLennan County, Texas	$83,946	8.6%
Nueces County, Texas	$85,024	9.7%
Henrico County, Virginia	$148,362	12.8%
Norfolk city, Virginia	$113,934	4.9%
Richmond city, Virginia	$131,072	3.7%
Virginia Beach city, Virginia	$154,230	8.3%
Spokane County, Washington	$131,383	12.1%
Yakima County, Washington	$126,089	5.7%
Kanawha County, West Virginia	$93,016	1.7%
Milwaukee County, Wisconsin	$117,096	3.2%
Racine County, Wisconsin	$129,386	9.2%

SOURCES: U.S. Census Bureau Manufacturing, Mining and Construction Statistics. County Building Permits 2000–2004. Washington, D.C.: U.S. Census Bureau, 2000–2006; U.S. Census Bureau. 2000 Decennial Census, County Housing Characteristics. Washington, D.C.: U.S. Census Bureau, 2000.
NOTES: House values from the 2000 U.S. census in 2000$. Permits share is the ratio of all housing permits issued 2000–2006 to the aggregate housing stock as of the year 2000.

This leaves 52 counties out of the 307 large counties analyzed here. They are listed in table A2-5. They have moderate elasticities of supply by definition, but closer inspection indicates that most of them are more like the inelastic group (the first group) than the other two groups. Many of them had average house values at or above $200,000 in the year 2000, but none have extremely high permitting rates (by definition). They are an indication that any such categorization scheme will have "close calls," but such counties are relatively few in number. We prefer to keep the differences between the elastic and inelastic groups as sharp as possible, and not count these counties as part of either one of those groups.

TABLE A2-5

LARGE COUNTIES WITH MODERATE ELASTICITIES OF SUPPLY

County name	Mean house value (2000$)	Permits share
Anchorage municipality, Alaska	$164,787	12.3%
Madison County, Alabama	$124,067	14.3%
Contra Costa County, California	$326,294	11.1%
Fresno County, California	$130,366	13.4%
San Bernardino County, California	$143,404	14.1%
San Luis Obispo County, California	$263,309	14.1%
Solano County, California	$199,986	12.2%
Tulare County, California	$121,698	14.2%
Boulder County, Colorado	$280,921	10.4%
Denver County, Colorado	$198,662	10.7%
Jefferson County, Colorado	$216,527	7.1%
Hartford County, Connecticut	$167,961	4.5%
Litchfield County, Connecticut	$200,213	6.4%
New Haven County, Connecticut	$172,932	4.0%
New London County, Connecticut	$170,844	6.6%
Cook County, Illinois	$196,573	5.2%
DuPage County, Illinois	$228,770	7.4%
Lake County, Illinois	$263,806	12.5%
Linn County, Iowa	$118,580	13.9%
Lafayette Parish, Louisiana	$113,840	13.4%
Anne Arundel County, Maryland	$198,641	9.2%
Howard County, Maryland	$228,755	12.6%
Bristol County, Massachusetts	$166,719	5.4%
Plymouth County, Massachusetts	$214,718	7.6%
Worcester County, Massachusetts	$169,659	7.6%
Oakland County, Michigan	$217,250	7.2%
Washtenaw County, Michigan	$201,293	10.8%
Hennepin County, Minnesota	$178,686	7.8%
Jackson County, Missouri	$104,920	13.3%
Jefferson County, Missouri	$104,619	14.4%
Rockingham County, New Hampshire	$185,748	10.1%
Cape May County, New Jersey	$184,579	13.1%
Hudson County, New Jersey	$182,864	7.8%

continued on next page

Table A2-5 continued

County name	Mean house value (2000$)	Permits share
Mercer County, New Jersey	$194,034	6.8%
Middlesex County, New Jersey	$183,934	6.2%
Passaic County, New Jersey	$211,271	2.9%
Bronx County, New York	$189,527	4.9%
Dutchess County, New York	$173,849	7.0%
Queens County, New York	$225,399	4.3%
Suffolk County, New York	$227,168	5.4%
Cumberland County, North Carolina	$99,668	14.4%
Butler County, Ohio	$133,715	13.3%
Clackamas County, Oregon	$234,349	11.4%
Multnomah County, Oregon	$188,654	9.1%
Bucks County, Pennsylvania	$193,755	7.6%
Chester County, Pennsylvania	$219,834	13.1%
Montgomery County, Pennsylvania	$200,102	6.8%
Knox County, Tennessee	$122,878	13.8%
Salt Lake County, Utah	$184,700	13.8%
King County, Washington	$277,717	10.9%
Kitsap County, Washington	$184,272	9.9%
Waukesha County, Wisconsin	$201,065	11.2%

SOURCES: U.S. Census Bureau Manufacturing, Mining and Construction Statistics. County Building Permits 2000–2004. Washington, D.C.: U.S. Census Bureau, 2000–2006; U.S. Census Bureau. 2000 Decennial Census, County Housing Characteristics. Washington, D.C.: U.S. Census Bureau, 2000.
NOTES: House values from the 2000 U.S. census in 2000$. Permits share is the ratio of all housing permits issued between 2000–2006 to the aggregate housing stock as of the year 2000.

Funding the Program:
Reforming the Home Mortgage Interest Deduction

The starting point for our proposal is that interest will be deductible only on the first $300,000 dollars of housing debt.[10] This cap ensures that the overwhelming majority of households would not feel any direct impact of this tax change whatsoever. Data from the most recent Survey of Consumer Finances in 2004 indicate that 4.3 percent of owner-occupied homes have total mortgage indebtedness in excess of $300,000, so fewer than one in twenty owners will find this change binding. This share translates into

3,074,500 individual units across the nation, according to the SCF. These large mortgages are also disproportionately held by the wealthiest people in society, so that the equity considerations are minor.[11] Moreover, since those holding these mortgages tend to be so wealthy, they are generally not people on the margin between owning and renting. Naturally, we recommend that the $300,000 cap be indexed to a reasonable price index.[12]

The second part of our plan then lifts the cap on mortgage interest deductibility for owners in all counties that do not have inelastic supplies of housing.[13] We acknowledge that there are credible arguments for not lifting the cap in these counties, too, as it is not at all clear why the government should be in the business of increasing the housing consumption of relatively wealthy people anywhere. However, our focus is on housing affordability, and we are confident that uncapping the home mortgage interest deduction in those areas will not make housing less affordable because there are little or no price effects from this deduction in elastic counties that are providing abundant housing.

The question of whether the low-demand counties should also face the mortgage cap is more difficult. Since these areas have both low prices and low construction levels, it is not so straightforward to determine whether they have elastic or inelastic housing supplies. In practice, house prices are so low in many of the counties in this third group that there will be little fiscal impact no matter whether the mortgage interest deduction is allowed or not. Hence, to err on the side of caution, we also recommend lifting the interest deduction cap in these markets, too.

Before getting to the financial details of this proposal, it should be noted that there is nothing novel about suggesting a cap on the amount of mortgage for which interest can be deducted. Currently, home mortgage debt in excess of $1 million cannot be deducted. The President's Advisory Panel on Federal Tax Reform also proposed a cap on mortgage deductibility, though it proposed that more, not less, mortgage interest be deductible in more expensive areas. We recognize the concerns that led them to their conclusion, but believe that efficiency concerns push in exactly the opposite direction, and they drive our recommendation. By allowing more mortgage interest deductibility in high-price areas, where housing supply is most restricted, the panel is essentially providing more demand-side subsidy in exactly the places where it will do the most harm in terms of housing affordability. We propose that the savings to the federal government be used to encourage more housing production in high-demand markets with limited supply. In addition, we want to tie the savings to new housing production in a way that is fiscally neutral.

To gain insight into how that process would work, we first need to compute the magnitude of tax revenues generated in the thirty-six large counties we classified as being in inelastic supply using the metrics discussed above.[14] To further simplify the analysis, we assume that house prices and mortgage levels remain unchanged in the face of the new policy. This allows us to easily estimate the amount of new revenue that will be produced by reducing the mortgage cap in these counties. The starting point for our calculation is the 2004 SCF, which provides excellent wealth data that allow us to clearly identify which owners have mortgage debt in excess of $300,000. It does not, however, provide any information on where these people live,[15] so we need to impute location across counties.

We know that high mortgage indebtedness occurs on high-priced homes, so our strategy simply is to allocate the just-over three million mortgages with outstanding balances above $300,000 to counties based on their share of homes valued at more than $1 million as reported in the 2000 census.[16] Los Angeles County, CA, has the largest share of homes valued above $1 million, at 8.3 percent, according to the census data. Hence, we allocated that county 255,793 of the 3,074,500 mortgages that the 2004 SCF indicated had balances of at least $300,000.[17] The first two columns of table A2-6 list the share and number of $300,000+ mortgages in each of the thirty-six large counties that we concluded are in inelastic supply. These figures show that there is substantial heterogeneity in exposure to these mortgages, with the majority of counties having very low shares and only a few such mortgages. There are fourteen counties with shares of these very large mortgages in excess of 1 percent, and each is part of a very high-price coastal market.

Next, we have to compute the amount of mortgage interest that the holders of these mortgages reasonably could expect to deduct. For this, we return to the 2004 SCF, which provides detailed interest rate data on these mortgages. To compute the annual amount of mortgage interest that is deductible, we multiply the interest rate times the outstanding balance above $300,000, controlling for the fact that current law already prohibits

deductions on mortgage indebtedness in excess of $1 million.[18] This calcu-
lation generates an average amount of deductible mortgage interest equal to
$7,188 per annum on these high-balance loans.[19] The aggregate deductible
mortgage interest from these large loans in each county is reported in column three of table A2-6.

Because mortgage interest is deductible and not a credit, the amount of
the tax expenditure involved depends upon the borrower's tax rate. Tax
rates are not known with certainty in any jurisdiction, and the tax bracket
for two earners with identical salaries can and does vary geographically—
there are sometimes large differences in state and local taxes—or depending upon where they are in the life cycle. To be conservative, we do not
assume that everyone with such a mortgage is in the top marginal bracket.
Rather, we presume that all borrowers are in the second-highest, or 33 percent, bracket. Multiplying deductible interest by 0.33 provides the amount
of taxes that no longer can be saved on these large loans. This amount is
provided in the fourth column of table A2-6. This figure reflects the amount
of new taxes the federal government receives that it would not have
received in the absence of our new mortgage deduction cap in inelastically
supplied housing markets.[20]

The final provision of our reform proposal for the home mortgage interest deduction in markets with inelastic housing supplies is that the tax revenues generated by this policy change (which equal the tax expenditures
recouped) be redistributed back to the counties to allow them to encourage
their localities to allow more housing construction.

Local governments do not impose restrictions on residential development out of spite. They are responding to the desires of their residents, who
perceive many costs associated with the growth that accompanies new
building. As we argued above, the prime beneficiaries of new development
in a locality are the outsiders who are able to move in, not the current residents. The goal of our policy is to provide the responsible local entities
with resources to compensate their residents for the downside of growth.
The problems and prospects for administering such a program are discussed more fully below. For the moment, the importance of this policy recommendation is that it turns what heretofore had been exclusively a
demand-side national subsidy into a supply-side program in the highest-
cost housing markets in inelastic supply.

An important and unresolved question is how many resources need to be provided for local government in inelastically supplied markets to allow more construction. We turn to the Mt. Laurel housing program in New Jersey for insight into this issue. Recall that this program requires communities to support the building of a certain amount of affordable housing. Importantly, communities that do not want to allow this housing within their own jurisdictions can pay a fee to avoid it. Recent data indicate that communities are paying at least $25,000 per housing unit to have the unit constructed elsewhere in the state. This is market data on willingness to pay to avoid new construction by (predominantly) suburban communities in New Jersey. We add a slight premium to this to arrive at a $30,000 figure for the resources that must be transferred to a community in order for it actually to permit the building of a single housing unit within its jurisdiction.

With this metric, we can determine whether the resources freed up by the lower cap on the mortgage interest deduction are significant enough to materially increase the amount of permitting in our inelastic counties. The last two columns of table A2-6 indicate that the answer is "yes" in many cases. The penultimate column reports the number of new housing units that could be permitted if all the tax savings were rebated to the county, which then "bought" new housing permits within its jurisdiction at a cost of $30,000 per unit. The final column reports the average annual permitting rate over the last seven years (2000–2006). In many places, including some of the highest-house-price counties in northern California, the amount of permitting could more than double based on our assumptions. The median value of the ratio of implied new homes to average annual permits is 0.67, with three-quarters of these thirty-six counties experiencing at least 35 percent increases in permitting activity. Essentially, while less than 5 percent of all mortgages nationwide are subject to our new mortgage cap, these mortgages are disproportionately held in these inelastic counties. Assuming we actually learn something about what it would take to allow new construction on the margin from the $30,000 that New Jersey suburban communities are willing to pay to avoid new construction, we would see a material increase in the flow of new housing in most inelastically supplied counties, given current production rates.

TABLE A2-6

LARGE COUNTIES WITH INELASTIC HOUSING SUPPLY—
MORTGAGE INTEREST CAP PROGRAM EFFECTS

County	Mortgage share	Number of mortgages
Alameda County, California	1.1%	34,000
Los Angeles County, California	8.3%	255,793
Marin County, California	1.8%	55,711
Monterey County, California	0.6%	18,094
Orange County, California	2.7%	83,238
San Diego County, California	2.0%	62,949
San Francisco County, California	2.2%	68,284
San Mateo County, California	3.5%	108,378
Santa Barbara County, California	1.1%	33,096
Santa Clara County, California	6.1%	186,074
Santa Cruz County, California	0.3%	10,110
Sonoma County, California	0.5%	16,769
Ventura County, California	0.4%	12,808
Fairfield County, Connecticut	3.1%	94,735
District of Columbia	0.4%	13,346
Honolulu County, Hawaii	0.4%	12,801
Montgomery County, Maryland	0.6%	19,316
Barnstable County, Massachusetts	0.2%	5,700
Essex County, Massachusetts	0.3%	8,619
Middlesex County, Massachusetts	1.1%	34,621
Norfolk County, Massachusetts	0.7%	20,075
Suffolk County, Massachusetts	0.4%	13,208
Bergen County, New Jersey	0.8%	24,560
Essex County, New Jersey	0.4%	12,518
Monmouth County, New Jersey	0.4%	12,946
Morris County, New Jersey	0.4%	12,325
Somerset County, New Jersey	0.3%	10,034
Union County, New Jersey	0.2%	5,900
Kings County, New York	0.9%	27,810
Nassau County, New York	1.7%	50,900
New York County, New York	5.1%	157,939
Richmond County, New York	0.1%	2,843
Rockland County, New York	0.1%	2,291
Westchester County, New York	2.0%	60,113
Arlington County, Virginia	0.0%	1,090
Fairfax County, Virginia	0.5%	15,327

SOURCES: U.S. Census of Population and Housing, 2000; Survey of Consumer Finances, 2004; authors' calculations.
NOTES: Mortgage share is imputed from the county's share of all homes in the nation valued in excess of $1,000,000. Number of mortgages is the mortgage share from column 1 times the 3,074,500 homes with mortgage indebtedness in excess of $300,000 (SCF). Annual aggregate deductible interest is the product

Annual aggregate deductible interest	Implied tax expenditure for 33% bracket	Implied new units	Average annual permits
$244,394,017	$80,650,026	2,688	4,480
$1,838,641,330	$606,751,639	20,225	21,121
$400,447,469	$132,147,665	4,405	643
$130,060,013	$42,919,804	1,431	1,263
$598,313,186	$197,443,351	6,581	9,554
$452,480,755	$149,318,649	4,977	14,542
$490,823,398	$161,971,721	5,399	1,945
$779,018,636	$257,076,150	8,569	1,341
$237,896,762	$78,505,932	2,617	1,210
$1,337,499,672	$441,374,892	14,712	5,886
$72,667,596	$23,980,307	799	742
$120,535,126	$39,776,591	1,326	2,275
$92,064,332	$30,381,230	1,013	3,268
$680,952,078	$224,714,186	7,490	2,271
$95,931,746	$31,657,476	1,055	1,660
$92,013,503	$30,364,456	1,012	2,967
$138,840,146	$45,817,248	1,527	4,298
$40,972,484	$13,520,920	451	1,410
$61,953,755	$20,444,739	681	2,162
$248,858,117	$82,123,179	2,737	3,667
$144,296,514	$47,617,850	1,587	1,986
$94,939,478	$31,330,028	1,044	1,406
$176,537,484	$58,257,370	1,942	2,138
$89,980,349	$29,693,515	990	2,231
$93,056,600	$30,708,678	1,024	2,609
$88,590,290	$29,234,796	974	1,904
$72,123,948	$23,800,903	793	1,450
$42,411,162	$13,995,683	467	1,068
$199,901,082	$65,967,357	2,199	6,032
$365,872,791	$120,738,021	4,025	1,217
$1,135,267,093	$374,638,141	12,488	6,242
$20,435,413	$6,743,686	225	2,039
$16,468,552	$5,434,622	181	525
$432,093,961	$142,591,007	4,753	1,713
$7,836,485	$2,586,040	86	1,038
$110,168,247	$36,355,522	1,212	5,023

of the number of mortgages from column 2 times the $7,188 annual interest imputed from the SCF. Implied tax expenditure for 33% bracket is the product of the annual aggregate deductible interest in column 3 times 0.33 (the assumed tax rate). Implied new units is the implied tax expenditure from column 4 divided by $30,000 (the assumed price of each additional permit). Average annual permits is the yearly average of all housing permits issued in the county between 2000–2006.

Reforming Supply-Side Policies:
Administering the New Home Mortgage Interest Deduction
Program in Counties with Inelastic Housing Supplies

We finally turn to our proposal about what to do with the revenues from reducing the home mortgage interest deduction in high-cost, inelastic areas. In those areas, supply is being severely restricted by local governments. A sensible program would use the home mortgage interest deduction funds to create incentives for localities to build. It would also ensure that these funds go directly to the local governments making the decisions about permitting, rather than to developers. Those localities can then use those funds to pay for schools or police or infrastructure, or the funding can be used to reduce taxes or to offset some of the social costs associated with new construction.

Enough new funding will be generated by the change in the home mortgage interest deduction that the potential impact of this program on the flow of new supply is large, as indicated by the figures reported above in table A2-6. However, there are substantial problems administering such a program at the national level. States differ wildly in their rules concerning the level of government that controls local land-use decisions, as well as the level of government responsible for different public services. For example, in the high-demand areas in Maryland that are close to Washington, DC, the county government is responsible both for land-use decisions and for spending on schools and other services. In the high-demand areas in Massachusetts that surround Boston, tiny localities are responsible for both land-use decisions and school spending. Consequently, there cannot be a uniform national policy that rewards communities that build more and penalizes ones that do not. The need to allow state-by-state variation requires a great deal of local knowledge that the federal government does not have. Hence, we propose that the onus be put on states to come up with a reasonable supply-side program.

One implementation strategy would require the states that face an increase in taxes from the restriction on the home mortgage interest deduction to propose a program that will then be evaluated, perhaps by a special committee appointed by the president. Each program can be different, but it will need to have certain specific characteristics.

First, it must provide money only for government services (including tax reductions) and only in the counties with owners who paid the increased mortgage taxes. In other words, if $1 million is raised by lowering the mortgage cap in Montgomery County, MD, then $1 million must be allocated to different areas within Montgomery County, and not to other counties within the state or to other nongovernmental recipients. Second, the program must direct funding as a function of the number of housing permits issued. Finally, the federal government will ensure that the program actually has an effect by tying payouts from the state to new production in the county.

As it will take some time for a state to develop an acceptable plan, tax revenues will accumulate before any program can be implemented. Hence, we further propose that no payouts occur for at least a year after the mortgage deduction is reduced, which will allow a significant buildup in the money that can be used to encourage new housing in inelastic areas. The first year's revenues can be used as part of any plan that is approved by the state. However, for states to receive further increases in revenues, they will need to show a substantial increase in permitting and construction.

In the first two years, we suggest that a 10 percent increase in permitting should be enough to show progress. Thus, to receive continuing funding in years two and three of the program, it is enough to show that permits have increased by 10 percent over the prior seven-year average (i.e., 2000–06 in our data).

After two years, however, the counties must reach a threshold which is determined by their existing building rate and the 10 percent permit share that we used as a cutoff for inelastic counties. That share is equivalent to a 1.42 percent annual permitting rate (10 percent/7years = 1.42). For a county to have made progress by year three, its building rate must have risen to the point where it has eliminated one-half of the distance between its prior rate and a 1.42 percent rate. That is, if the county was building an average of 1 percent per year, it must have reached 1.21 percent per year. This makes the increase more onerous for those counties that were initially producing less housing, which seems appropriate. If this amount is less than a 10 percent increase, then the county's construction level must continue to be at least 10 percent more than its baseline construction level.

If the county's construction level reaches 1.42 percent for at least four years, then it ceases to qualify as an inelastic county and it gets removed from the program. Any surplus in the program, however, will remain with the federal government in case the county again becomes less elastic. It is possible that governments may end up preferring the money transferred from the program to resuming the home mortgage interest deduction, and this may lead them to oppose building that moves above the 1.42 percent threshold. If this type of behavior appears to be important, then it may be necessary to slightly alter the incentive scheme accordingly.

Subject to these constraints, the states would have the freedom to come up with their own uses of the funds. As of today, we classify only eight states as having inelastic counties: California, Connecticut, Hawaii, Maryland, Massachusetts, New Jersey, New York, and Virginia.[21] Of these eight states, three have only one inelastic county (Connecticut, Hawaii, and Maryland), and Virginia has only two counties that are inelastic. As such, four of these states are really dealing with a relatively modest problem of encouraging new construction in a relatively geographically constrained area. The four states that contain the bulk of the inelastic counties are California, Massachusetts, New York, and New Jersey. These are the areas that have the biggest problems with new construction and where there are the biggest gains for building new housing. New Jersey already has a program in place that attempts to generate new construction. That program could easily provide the outline for further attempts to use the mortgage interest deduction to build more housing.

In places like Maryland, where county governments are strong and have both the power to permit new construction and responsibility over major public services, an appropriate program might just pass along the government funding (presuming it is available) to the counties themselves. In other words, Montgomery County receives the home mortgage interest deduction money if, and only if, it increases construction by 10 percent in the first two years of the program; and then if it increases construction to the point where it halves the distance between the current base and the 1.42 percent cutoff in the years after that. The state would channel the money that it gets directly to the counties.

In states where the counties have little power over new construction, the system would have to be different, since the federal payout depends on construction at the county level, and individual localities control only a small amount of construction within the county. The most natural program would have a points system, where points are allocated on the basis of new construction. Bonus points could be allowed for housing that is particularly friendly to low-income individuals or for high-density construction, at the discretion of the state. There could also be some recognition that it might be harder to build in areas that are already dense, so more points could be given for building in denser areas.

If the overall construction target level is reached, the cash is then shared among the localities on the basis of the number of points that they have accumulated. Places that built more will get more money, which creates an incentive for more construction. The exact point system could reflect local needs and the particular desires of the state itself, as long as the money is then allocated to local governments to meet their own spending needs.

The federal government can be relatively flexible in accepting proposed point systems, because the overall funding will be tied to new construction. If the program works, then the state will get its funding. If there is little new construction, then the funding will stop, and the state will need to come up with a new plan. By tying the funding to actual results, there is less need to micromanage the point system from Washington, DC. These systems are appropriately designed and implemented by states, not Washington, because states have the incentive to avoid a funding cutoff.

Notes

Introduction

1. The commission's analysis is based on data from the 1999 American Housing Survey (AHS). The Department of Housing and Urban Development uses this 30 percent standard, too.

2. See Glaeser and Gyourko (2006) for the details behind these calculations.

3. See LexisNexis Municipal Codes (2008) for the Marin County municipal codes.

Chapter 1: How Do We Know
When Housing Is "Affordable"?

1. Programs such as the LIHTC and Section 8 vouchers cannot avoid introducing some inequality among the poor themselves. Because they are not fully funded mandates, inequality is created simply because some households and not others are lucky enough to receive a voucher or to occupy a subsidized unit.

2. This is a central principle of modern urban economics that was introduced by Sherwin Rosen (1979) and Roback (1982). Unfortunately, it has never influenced the discussion of housing affordability.

3. Our assumption that the annual user costs of living in a home are 10 percent of house value is certainly debatable, but this figure is not extreme, either. The true number varies by income because of mortgage interest deductibility, but 10 percent is well within the range of annual user costs estimated by Poterba (1992), Poterba and Sinai (2008), and other studies of this issue. Reasonable changes in the user cost figure also have no impact on our basic point: using an affordability measure that looks at housing costs relative to income is not useful for cross-metropolitan comparisons.

4. Such a market is characterized by constant returns to scale in economic terms. This does appear to be the case in most markets. See Gyourko and Saiz (2006) for recent evidence supporting the existence of competitive housing construction markets with constant returns to scale.

Chapter 2: The State of American Housing

1. These figures are from the U.S. Census Bureau, which provides data on the characteristics of new residential construction. See U.S. Census Bureau 2008.

2. Note that the data used in figure 2-3 include only households with heads less than fifty-five years old. If more elderly households are included in the sample, those in the bottom quartile of the income distribution live in the largest (not the smallest) units. The difference arises because many retirees, who report little or no income, live in large housing units they purchased many years in the past.

3. The sample sizes for some categories (e.g., renters in the top quartile of the income distribution and owners in the bottom quartile of income distribution) are small in some years, so sampling variation could account for some of the changes depicted in this figure. In addition, the AHS data on unit size are not continuous in nature, but are reported in interval form. Hence, changes across intervals may overstate the true change in square footage. The important point to be taken from the figure is that there is no evidence that poorer renters or owners are consuming less space, absolutely or relative to the rich.

4. Part of the reason for this is that, unlike Europeans, many modest-income Americans live in single-family housing in suburban areas.

5. The question about whether plumbing is complete is not even asked in the most recent census, presumably because there is not any interesting variation in the answers.

6. This is not solely due to the rise of American suburbs in the post-war era. Gyourko (forthcoming) documents that the quality of central city housing stocks is much improved, too.

7. While beyond the scope of this study, this is an interesting pattern that could be due to rising immigration. In any event, it is worthy of closer analysis in other research.

8. There are good reasons why people want to rent in the first place and why those who live in multifamily dwellings rent. Rental contracts avoid the fixed costs associated with buying a house, and preserve mobility for those who may need to move for personal or job-related reasons. In particular, the young and those living in declining labor markets might wish to move to a more productive market to improve their life chances. In addition, the subprime mortgage market problems starkly illustrate that owning can be risky, especially for those without sufficient capital resources to withstand turbulence in the credit markets. Finally, having one owner for each roof appears to solve what economists refer to as agency problems, which arise when multiple owners have to collectively manage shared infrastructure.

9. House prices are in constant 2000 dollars and represent the typical quality home in each metropolitan area as indicated in the 2000 census. Incomes also are in constant 2000 dollars and are per capita averages from the Bureau of Economic Analysis.

10. House prices are the same as those used in figure 2-9. The mean January temperature is a thirty-year average taken from the 2000 *County and City Data Book.*

11. This is consistent with the pattern for virtually all manufactured durable goods. Housing is a very durable good, and homebuilders have brought efficient manufacturing practices to the industry, resulting in no rise in real construction costs over the past quarter century.

Chapter 4: Current Policies—Price and Quantity Controls

1. These statewide bans are understandable in political and economic terms in the following sense. While rent control may benefit some current tenants, they harm many other people in the state who currently live outside the rent-controlled city but who might like to move to it.

2. Arnott (1995) is right that second-generation rent control is less harmful in this respect, but we are far more pessimistic about the value of such controls than his study. As argued above, there is no reason to believe that control regimes permitting rents to be negotiated freely between landlords and new tenants will actually redistribute resources between parties. Nor is it at all clear that the front-loading of rents that should result in this setting will benefit the young and the credit constrained, both likely to be renters. These second-generation policies also could create incentives for lower investment by landlords who rationally may fear some future set of controls. They also artificially reduce mobility of renters, which is not a desirable outcome. While it should certainly be possible for landlords and tenants to sign multiyear contracts that limit rent increases, it is hard to see the case for the state to mandate such contracts, which is what rent stabilization effectively does.

Far more damaging would be a policy like that currently under consideration in Boston, which would encourage collective bargaining over rents. The proposed legislation in Boston supports denying future building permits to landlords who do not bargain in good faith with tenants' organizations. This represents a novel shift in the attempt to create oases of below-market rents. Proponents of this policy make a false analogy with collective bargaining over employment contracts in the labor market. The analogy does not hold because the heart of a labor strike involves employees withholding what is legally theirs (i.e., their time and effort), and they do not get paid while on strike. In the rental market, the landlord, not the tenant, is selling services (use of a property) in exchange for money. The closest analogy to a labor strike would be many small landlords, each providing space for a single large tenant, collectively refusing to sell space unless the tenant agreed to more concessions. Collective bargaining over rents has all the disadvantages of traditional rent control, plus the added costs associated with bargaining. One of the great advantages of a decentralized market is that it requires little from its participants.

Prices are posted and people decide whether to buy. This is currently how the rental system works. Once this system is transformed into a bargaining scenario with lengthy debates and plenty of opportunity for bringing in the help of government and lawyers, the low-cost market will require large amounts of effort from everyone. Both landlords and tenants will pay dearly if many cities ever decide to switch from a market system to confrontational bargaining.

3. The case for using earlier controls is that later controls are themselves endogenously determined by minimum lot size, and controlling for them may underestimate the true effect of minimum lot size.

4. While it is possible that the relationship between permitting and minimum lot size reflects omitted variables that simultaneously affect both variables, there are good reasons to suspect that a significant portion of the observed relationship is causal. First, the results for minimum lot sizes do control for a bevy of town-level characteristics, including historical density levels, educational and industrial variables, and distance to Boston. Second, minimum lot sizes have a strong effect in the 1990s even though those lot sizes were generally determined decades earlier. If lot sizes reflected a common effect that changes over time, then presumably the correlation between minimum lot sizes and new construction should be declining substantially over time. Third, if regulations are applied as written, minimum lot sizes should have a very direct impact on the amount of new construction. As such, the causal interpretation that bigger minimum lot sizes reduce construction is extremely natural and far simpler than any alternative story.

5. For the underlying data from the survey, as well as a paper and data appendix describing the sample and variables in more detail, see Gyourko, Saiz, and Summers (2008b).

6. House prices for 2005 are scaled from 2000 census means using the appreciation from the OFHEO price index for each metropolitan area.

7. If one does not exclude the five metropolitan areas with very low house prices, the simple correlation is −0.30, so it remains reliably negative, if somewhat less strong.

8. The interested reader should see Ihlanfeldt and Burge (2006a, 2006b) for more detail on impact fees for single-family and multifamily construction.

9. See Glaeser, Gyourko, and Saiz (forthcoming, tables 6, 7) for more detail.

10. For example, if requiring that 30 percent of the units in a project be affordable reduces the profitability of the development by 30 percent, then this would reduce new supply by 30 percent if the overall elasticity of supply is 1.

11. See *Southern Burlington County N.A.A.C.P v. Township of Mount Laurel*, 67 NJ 151 (1975) for the case itself. Hughes and Vandoren (1990) and Kirp, Dwyer, and Rosenthal (1995) provide useful context and detail on the ruling and the housing program it spawned.

Chapter 5: Other Interventions in
Housing Markets—Taxes and Subsidies

1. The implicit income flow reflects the opportunity cost of not renting out your home and equals the rent you could have charged someone to live in the house. In economic terms, the true subsidy arises from the nontaxation of the return to equity in one's home. See Gyourko and Sinai (2003) for the analysis underpinning that conclusion.

2. See Harvey Rosen (1979) for a classic analysis. Bruce and Holtz-Eakin (1997), Capozza, Green, and Hendershott (1996), and Glaeser and Shapiro (2003) provide more recent investigations into how the tax code functions in these regards.

3. The largest component of the $147 billion figure is about $69 billion in tax expenditures for the mortgage interest deduction. Direct expenditures go toward voucher programs, public housing, and a variety of programs intended to subsidize rental costs for low- and moderate-income families.

4. The analysis is based on data from the 2000 census. The true subsidy differs from the amount of federal tax expenditures for a variety of reasons. Sinai and Gyourko (2004) compute estimates by comparing the current tax treatment of home-owners to their tax treatment if housing were like any other asset, with owners treated as if they were rental landlords. The subsidy itself equals the difference in taxes paid under the two tax regimes. See the paper for more details.

5. These data are for the three-county region (San Francisco County, San Mateo County, and Marin County) defining the San Francisco primary metropolitan statistical area (PMSA). The price is for 2006 and is for a home with the quality of the median home in the 2000 census. There has been very little variation in permitting, as the maximum number of housing permits issued in any year since 1980 is only 6,907 for this metropolitan area. Hence, the San Francisco PMSA has been stingy with housing permits for the past three decades.

6. The specific house price figure is $161,706 and is for the median quality home in the 2000 census. The smallest number of permits issued in any year in the Atlanta metropolitan area was 11,982; the maximum was 74,007.

7. In economic terms, housing is said to be in inelastic supply when the supply schedule is steeply sloped. Ever higher prices do not bring forth many new units, which is consistent with binding restrictions on building.

8. This graph assumes a given per-unit subsidy. While not literally true, it well captures the spirit of how sellers of homes reap the benefit of tax-code-related subsidies to homeowners in markets like San Francisco. In economic terms, the economic incidence of the subsidy falls on sellers of homes in markets with relatively inelastic supplies and relatively elastic demands.

9. See Saks (2008) for an overview of the literature on supply elasticities and local land-use and building regulation.

10. Housing is said to be in elastic supply in this market.

11. Our discussion has abstracted from how the subsidies are financed, but even if one assumes a proportional financing scheme, the transfers to owners in coastal markets still are large. See Gyourko and Sinai (2003) for those details.

12. Previously, Fannie Mae had been a government agency, established in the 1930s.

13. Both studies find that GSE debt yields are about twenty-five to thirty basis points below those on highly rated, AA bonds issued in the private banking sector. The cost advantage goes up to eighty basis points if the comparison is made with respect to lower-rated, BBB bonds. Both sets of authors do their best to control for differences in the characteristics of the debt issuances, but all empirical work like this remains subject to some specification error. The interested reader should see Ambrose and Warga (2002) and Nothaft, Pearce, and Stevanovic (2002) and the cites therein for more detail on the underlying econometric strategy.

14. Because the number of homeowners is very large, this difference sums to a fairly large number, but it still pales compared to the value of the underlying asset base. There are about eighty million owner-occupiers in the United States, although not all their homes are financed with conforming loans that could be purchased or securitized by Fannie Mae or Freddie Mac. For every ten million such loans, annual debt service payments are $3.96 billion less than they would be otherwise according to these estimates. Thus, if we were to assume that half of the ownership base received part of the subsidy to Fannie Mae and Freddie Mac, mortgage payment savings would be $15.84 billion lower each year. That is not a small number in absolute terms, but it is not large when compared to the $20.6 trillion of real estate owned by the household sector.

15. Heretofore, we have deliberately avoided the issue of whether Fannie Mae and Freddie Mac should be more tightly regulated to control systemic risk to the financial system arising from large mortgage holdings in their portfolio. Jaffee (2003) convincingly argues that potentially large interest rate risk exists even with the hedging strategies of the two GSEs. The recent financial crises at both GSEs highlight the different risks associated with their credit guarantees. Given all this, and the fact that the component of the subsidy passed through to borrowers largely goes to non-poor homeowners, we do not see a justification for the increased systemic risk to the financial system that arises from the implicit default insurance provided Fannie Mae and Freddie Mac.

16. This number also includes units designated for the elderly, the disabled, and the American Indian population, so not all are part of the traditional public housing construction program.

17. An Abt Associates Inc. (2006) study for the Department of Housing and Urban Development reports 985,560 tax-credit-financed units delivered to the market between 1995 and 2004. Over the same time period, 2,938,200 privately owned multifamily units were started, where multifamily is defined as representing buildings with five or more units, according to the data in the table "New Privately Owned Housing Units Started (Annual Data)" available on the Census Bureau web site at

www.census.gov/const/compann.pdf. Even if one includes the nearly 130,000 apartments produced in small two- to four-unit structures, LIHTC unit production still amounts to more than 32 percent of all private rental construction over the decade. By any metric, this has become a very large program, but it is not the only production-based program. See the U.S. General Accounting Office (2002) and Olsen (2003) for a description of other, smaller production-based programs. These include HOPE VI, which subsidizes the rehabilitation of distressed public housing units; Section 8 New Construction/Substantial Rehabilitation; Section 202, which targets housing units for the elderly; Section 811, which does the same for disabled people; and Section 515, which is geographically focused on financing construction in rural areas.

18. These data are from Danter Company (2008). Danter is a consultant to developers and investors in LIHTC projects. Because it takes time to build housing, especially larger multi-unit structures, the number of units delivered typically lags behind the number authorized. In addition, there is a flow of credits for ten years, so the total resources being dedicated to the program by the federal government are roughly ten times these amounts (and those in table 5-5).

19. There often are other subsidies from other sources such as state or local governments. These can range from loans at below-market interest rates to outright grants of land. Recent research by Eriksen and Rosenthal (2007) reports that subsidy rates can vary from 30 to 91 percent of construction costs under different conditions. The cost of the subsidy is discussed later in the chapter.

20. Specific income restrictions are determined for a household of four people, with adjustments made for different household sizes.

21. This is an increase from the initial fifteen-year eligibility requirement, so not all LIHTC buildings in existence must stay eligible for three decades, and some no longer have to stay eligible.

22. For example, the threshold for a one-person household is presumed to be 70 percent of that for a four-person household. The analogous figures for two- and three-person families are 80 and 90 percent, respectively. Threshold incomes are adjusted up, by eight percentage points per family member, above four. See Olsen (2003) for the details.

23. The lowest Very Low Income level for any county in 2005 was $18,250. Generally speaking, values below $20,000 are confined to counties that are not part of metropolitan areas. Within metropolitan areas, the maximum income levels for program participation are at least $25,000. HUD posts various data on its web site at http://www.huduser.org/datasets/lihtc.html.

24. The $960 monthly rent in Columbus, OH, is computed as follows. Multiplying the $32,000 Very Low Income level for Franklin County in 2005 by 1.2 yields a 60th percentile income of $38,400. Multiplying this figure by 0.3 yields the maximum annual rent of $11,520 that this family can pay out of pocket. Dividing by twelve generates the $960 monthly rent noted in the text. A complicating factor is that maximum rents also are set based on the expected number of residents in

different-sized units. This is termed the "expected occupancy." Studio apartments are expected to have one person living in them, while four-bedroom units are expected to have six people living in them. And maximum income levels are adjusted downward for smaller households (e.g., the maximum income for a single-person household is 70 percent of that for a four-person household) and upward for larger households (e.g., the maximum income for a six-person household is 16 percent higher than that for a four-person household). Maximum rents for given sized apartments are based on expected occupancy, regardless of the number of people actually living in them. Thus, the $960 rent amount would be about the maximum that could be charged for a three- or four-bedroom apartment occupied by a family of four in a LIHTC project in Columbus, OH. The computation is similar for San Francisco County.

25. Wallace (1995) noted that the fraction of Very Low Income families in LIHTC units was about one-third of that in public housing and Section 8 New Construction projects.

26. The data are from Danter Company (2006).

27. Those six areas were Boston, MA; Chicago, IL; Brooklyn, NY; Manhattan-Bronx, NY; Los Angeles, CA; and Philadelphia, PA. See Cummings and DiPasquale (1999, 271, table 3).

28. Interestingly, one-third of the subsidies on the LIHTC projects analyzed derived from sources other than tax credits. However, these figures do not include any tenant-based subsidies (i.e., from vouchers). They include only project-based subsidies.

29. For more detail, see U.S. Government Accounting Office (2002, table 3 in appendix 1). In addition, the ratio of the estimated subsidy to total development costs is 70 percent in the GAO study, a figure that is very similar to that estimated by Cummings and DiPasquale (1999) for the early years of the program.

30. More specifically, the GAO compares costs for a one-bedroom unit, assuming the average incomes of the tax credit and voucher households were the same and that both groups of tenants paid the same percentage of their incomes in rent (U.S. GAO 2002, 29).

31. The underlying estimation involves a difficult econometric problem because it is likely that the number of subsidized units is correlated with unobserved determinants of housing demand, resulting in biased estimates of the extent of crowd-out. See Sinai and Waldfogel (2005) for more on this. Our interpretation of this literature is that the crowd-out effect is large, although it does not seem feasible to distinguish between these two estimates.

32. Baum-Snow and Marion (2008) also report evidence consistent with a high degree of crowd-out. The study's table 2 shows that the LIHTC program is producing units with rents at or above market rates in most cases. Even in relatively high-income areas, nearly two-thirds of apartments in the private market had rents below LIHTC-regulated levels in 2000. In the poorest census tracts analyzed, the market rate was below the regulated rent level 85 percent of the time.

33. That analysis, especially what is represented in figure 5-1, assumes a per-unit subsidy to all home buyers in the market. While that assumption is not literally true for owners, it is much less so in the case of apartment buildings, where subsidized construction is no more than one-third the share of new production in any given year.

34. There literally would be no benefit to renters in the form of lower rents, even in markets like San Francisco that are in inelastic supply, in the following situation. Providing a per-unit subsidy to select builders will have no effect on the long-run, equilibrium rent in a market if all firms are the same in the sense that they face identical U-shaped, long-run average cost curves, their input prices do not vary with the size of the market, and some unsubsidized firms remain in the industry in the long run. The equilibrium rent is determined by the minimum long-run average cost of production for unsubsidized firms in this case. The subsidy to the lucky firms in the program allows them to earn higher profits and there are fewer unsubsidized firms in equilibrium. The analysis would be materially different if all unsubsidized firms were forced out of the market, but that is not consistent with industry evidence. In addition, changes in input prices as the industry expands complicate the analysis, but do not alter the conclusion in a fundamental way. Given that the industry is characterized by constant returns to scale, this point is something of a technicality, in any event.

35. Technically, this program replaced the Section 23 program, which was passed in 1965 and allowed local public housing authorities for the first time to lease units in unsubsidized, private apartment buildings. See Olsen (2003) for more detail on the history of tenant-based subsidy programs in the United States.

36. The data are from U.S. Department of Housing and Urban Development (2007).

37. These examples are indicative of the payment required by HUD, but there are qualifications and exceptions that are likely to change the amounts an actual family would have to pay (e.g., due to expected occupancy for a three-bedroom unit).

38. Susin (2002) also considers the impact of the voucher program on low-income renter households as a group. This issue is relevant because vouchers are not a mandate and not all eligible households receive them. Thus, if vouchers raise rents on units occupied by low-income households, the loss to those families not receiving vouchers could be larger than the direct benefits of the vouchers to the families that receive them. Susin (2002) concludes that vouchers do actually result in a net loss to low-income households as a group. This result echoes the argument made by Apgar (1990) that the cost effectiveness of voucher programs was overestimated because they had been introduced when the overall rental market was weak.

39. Once again, we are hesitant to employ the simple graphical analysis that presumes a per-unit subsidy for all demanders in a market. The voucher program is not a mandate, so there are many poor families who are not recipients. That type of analysis would conclude that there are minimal effects on rents in markets with flat (elastic) supplies, but that rents would be increased by the presence of vouchers in markets with steep (inelastic) supplies.

40. An examination of the formula for allocating vouchers across markets (often metropolitan areas, but smaller geographies apply within large metropolitan areas) indicates that many are issued in markets with inelastic supplies of housing. The elements of the allocation formula include the number of renter households, the number of renter households in poverty, the number of renter households living in crowded units (defined as more than one person per room), the number of poor renter households in old buildings (defined as being constructed before 1940), the number of renter households paying high rents (defined as involving more than 30 percent of household income), and a couple of measures of vacancy shortage variables so that areas with low vacancy rates receive more vouchers. Housing markets with inelastic supply sides are likely to have very high house prices and thus many renters. They also often have fairly high poverty rates, as well as older housing stocks, so that the formula is likely to lead to significant voucher allocations to inelastically supplied markets. This presents an endogeneity problem that is difficult for Susin (2002) to deal with, but it still is consistent with at least some of the benefits of vouchers being passed along to landlords in the form of higher rents.

Conclusion

1. This fact makes clear that there are no excess profits for the marginal builder in these markets. Indeed, one of the unattractive features of land-use regulations is the wasteful expenditures that need to be made on lobbyists and lawyers to get a project through the approval process in a highly regulated market. Risk is higher, too, which can materially increase the carry costs of capital invested in the deal. Political savvy, not just excellent engineering skills, is needed to be a successful builder in these types of markets.

2. This externality does not exist if communities are maximizing land values and if they have no monopoly power. In this case, communities are essentially firms selling their wares, and in a competitive market they face the right incentives if they are trying to maximize profits. However, the democratic process in most areas does not particularly resemble land-value maximization. A majority vote on each new project, without transfers across voters, will yield far too little construction relative to the social optimum. Glaeser and Ward (2006) find that there is far too little development in many areas relative to land-value maximization.

3. For those who want to better understand the economics of why this is so, see the discussion in appendix 1, which builds on the analysis of the impact of the home mortgage interest deduction program in chapter 5.

4. Once again, we refer the interested reader to appendix 1 for more detail on the underlying economics behind these conclusions.

5. That is, the conventional view in economics is that a policy which provides $100 to buyers of cars fundamentally is the same as one that provides $100 to

sellers of cars. Housing subsidies are an exception to this rule because they involve developers, not sellers.

6. A better case can be made for subsidizing rehabilitation in low-cost, declining areas, but we still oppose this use of federal funds. In principle, positive externalities may well arise from renovating dilapidated buildings. However, accurately assessing which rehabilitated subsidized buildings will generate externalities that justify significant public expense is almost impossible. The only thing that we can be sure of is that subsidizing construction in any form in declining regions will lead to more supply in those regions. More cheap housing will disproportionately attract relatively poorer families (Glaeser and Gyourko 2005), and it is hard to see why the federal government would want to encourage greater concentrations of the poor in declining, low-cost housing markets.

7. In a sense, we are recommending a Pigovian subsidy that encourages communities to be more open to development.

8. There are more low-demand counties with very low permitting rates and very low house prices. Table A2-4 lists each of these 118 counties. Note that this leaves only 13 percent (52 out of our 307 large-county sample) undefined. Thus, our classification procedures are able to readily define most counties into one of the three relevant categories listed.

9. Reducing the deductibility of local property taxes might also be desirable, but we ignore that issue here.

Appendix 2

1. We recognize that the mortgage interest deduction is not needed in markets with flexible or elastic housing supplies, as they do not suffer from any fundamental affordability crisis. However, we wish to focus on policy changes in areas with real affordability issues. And, as noted above, we presume the mortgage interest deduction cannot be eliminated in total: given the potentially large wealth effects such a draconian change might engender, it is not at all clear to us that such a policy would be advisable. At the very least, it would require a very long phase-in period. Caps on interest deductibility are likely to be much less controversial politically, especially given that one already exists at $1 million.

2. While homeowners habitually overestimate the value of their homes, the errors in valuation typically are not systematically correlated with other significant variables (Goodman and Ittner 1992). There are other series on sales prices compiled by the National Association of Realtors, which report average sales prices for new and existing homes in many metropolitan areas on a quarterly basis. These data suffer from the fact that neither existing homes nor new homes sold are representative of the total stock of homes in an area. Moreover, these data are not available at the county level or for all markets in the United States. The OFHEO repeat sales index is available for

a large number of metropolitan areas, but not for individual counties. Repeat sales indexes are a very effective means of updating prices because they control for quality changes in the stock of homes sold. However, they can be used only to compare changes in house prices, not overall levels of prices. We do not use the OFHEO series in this work, but we suspect it will be useful for updating census price figures, at least for the subset of counties included in the index. We do not believe that rapid updating is necessary in any event. Despite local booms and busts, it remains true that some areas of the country have reliably higher levels of demand than others.

3. Technically speaking, this is not the top 10 percent of counties, because we have data on only 3,043 of the 3,141 counties in the U.S. The ninety-eight counties for which we do not have complete data are all rural and spread across sixteen states, mostly in the Deep South and the Great Plains. They are very small in terms of population and housing units, with the mean population being under sixty-two hundred and the average number of housing units in them being less than three thousand. Permit data are not available for these counties, so we cannot use them in our analysis. Of the 307 counties that constitute our top 10 percent in terms of housing units, the minimum number of units is 74,285. The mean is 238,699.

4. We recognize that normalizing the level of permits by the overall number of housing units can be misleading in some cases. For example, consider two counties that are of equal physical size. Assume that one county has 1 million homes and has added an extra 100,000 homes over a five-year period. Consider another county that contains 10,000 homes and has added 1,000 homes over a five-year period. Both have increased supply by 10 percent of their preexisting stocks, but the county with few existing homes is clearly supplying far less housing. This is a primary reason we focus our analysis on large counties, where large percentages translate into large absolute numbers. In addition, scaling by land area is far from perfect. Urban economists long have associated greater physical density with high prices because of agglomeration economies that are not necessarily associated with housing supply conditions. And, as our analysis documents, scaling by the market stock well serves our purposes.

5. Simply regressing average house value on the permit issuance share of the existing stock finds a significantly negative coefficient on the permit variable. The estimate implies that an increase of 0.1 (10 percent) in the permit share variable is associated with a $14,000 lower mean house price. The underlying regression estimate is Mean House Value = $180,955($7,395) − $140,058($45,931) × Permit Issuance Share, $R^2 = 0.03$, number of observations = 307.

6. Recall that we are using data from the 2000 census with prices in 2000 dollars. The OFHEO price index for the United States rose by 77 percent in nominal terms from the first quarter of 2000 through the first quarter of 2007 (the latest period for which data are available nationally). In today's terms, this translates into a price cutoff of just over $400,000 ($230,000 × 1.77 = $407,100). Hence these are very high-priced counties, indeed.

7. The average house price across all 3,064 counties for which we have complete data is $103,419. We do not believe this is a relevant benchmark because of likely quality differences in the stock of housing across heavily populated versus lightly populated counties. Housing quality in the larger counties probably is much higher.

8. There has been a 17.1 percent increase in the Consumer Price Index from 2000 to 2006.

9. There are only three counties we categorize as having elastic supplies that also have average house values above $230,000, and none is above the mean for the inelastic counties. They are Placer County, CA, Collier County, FL, and Fulton County, GA.

10. Our proposal interprets housing debt broadly and collectively. That is, it applies to all indebtedness collateralized by one's home, no matter the precise legal definition of the debt contract. This is to prevent owners from designing multiple $299,999 debt contracts to finance their homes.

11. The mean total income for all owners in the SCF sample is $89,051. This is less than 30 percent of the $308,127 average total income for the subset of owners with more than $300,000 in debt collateralized by one's home.

12. One possible price index is the Consumer Price Index. Alternatively, the mortgage cap could be indexed to national trends in housing prices described by the OFHEO price index.

13. This policy is made particularly simple in order to keep the administrative costs low. It is possible to have a more continuous policy in which the mortgage cap rises gradually with the amount of new production. That strategy would not create such a clear divide between elastic and inelastic regions, which probably more closely reflects reality in markets. It would, however, make the tax code far more complicated than our more simple proposal. Of course, if a county begins to produce more housing, then it can be reclassified from inelastic to elastic. Indeed, our hope is that this feature of our proposal will encourage people who currently oppose new construction in inelastic regions to see new building more favorably.

14. There are only seven other counties classified as inelastic among the more than three thousand nationwide. Hence, these thirty-six large counties account for almost all the population that will be affected. The seven other counties are San Benito County, CA; Hinsdale County, CO; Clear Creek County, CO; Monroe County, FL; Hunterdon County, FL; Putnam County, NY; and Falls Church city, VA.

15. This is done to protect the confidentiality of the survey respondents, who reveal much financial detail in their answers.

16. The census asks each owner to self-report the value of his or her home by placing it into one of nearly twenty intervals, with a top code of $1 million.

17. Experimenting with different allocation schemes based on homes valued at (say) $750,000 or more does not change our results in any material way.

18. To keep things simple, the algebra is as follows. Annual Mortgage Interest (AMI) = Interest Rate (i) × Excess Mortgage Balance (EMI), where EMI is the amount

above $300,000 with a cap at $700,000. The cap reflects the fact that interest already is not deductible on balances in excess of $1 million. We use the mean interest rate on the first loans on the properties in making the calculation. About 10 percent of the high-indebtedness homes have a second mortgage, and just over 1 percent have a third loan on the property. Interest rate data are sparser on these junior mortgages, but the available data do show they have higher rates, as expected. Hence, our calculation is underestimating mortgage interest being paid in about 10 percent of the cases.

19. The current million-dollar cap does matter. If that were not in place, our calculation shows that deductible annual mortgage interest would have been $9,530.

20. We both hope and believe that there will be a behavioral response to this policy change, so the actual tax change will be less than the amounts reported below. However, these calculations still provide a useful benchmark for the total amount of new tax revenues available.

21. The District of Columbia is also classified as having inelastic housing supply, but given its idiosyncratic government structure, it may be desirable to remove DC from the program or have Congress directly act on permitting there. Some may wonder why markets in southern Florida in particular are not included, given the dramatic price increases seen there in recent years. One reason is that our price data are from the 2000 census, which predates much of their recent appreciation. The other is that these markets are not supply constrained in any fundamental sense, as they tend to permit units at high rates. Because consistently high prices require strong demand and restricted supply, this suggests a correction is coming in those markets.

References

Abt Associates Inc. 2006. *HUD national Low Income Housing Tax Credit (LIHTC) database: Projects placed in service through 2004.* Report prepared for the U.S. Department of Housing and Urban Development. Washington, DC: U.S. Department of Housing and Urban Development.

Ambrose, Brent and Arthur Warga. 2002. Measuring potential GSE funding advantages. *Journal of Real Estate Finance and Economics* 25, no. 2/3: 129–50.

Apgar, William. 1990. Which housing policy is best? *Housing Policy Debate* 1, no. 1: 1–32.

Arnott, Richard. 1995. Time for revisionism on rent control? *Journal of Economic Perspectives* 9, no. 1: 99–120.

Auletta, Ken. 1979. *The streets were paved with gold.* New York: Random House.

Barzel, Yoram. 1974. A theory of rationing by waiting. *Journal of Law and Economics* 17, no. 1: 73–95.

Baum-Snow, Nathaniel and Justin Marion. 2008. The effects of Low Income Housing Tax Credit developments on neighborhoods. Working Paper, Economics Department, Brown University.

Bruce, Donald and Douglas Holtz-Eakin. 1999. Apocalypse now? Fundamental tax reform and residential housing values. Working Paper No. W6282, National Bureau of Economic Research, Cambridge, MA.

Capozza, Dennis, Richard Green, and Patric Hendershott. 1996. Taxes, mortgage borrowing, and residential land prices. In *Economic effects of fundamental tax reform*, ed. Henry Aaron and William Gale, 171–210. Washington, DC: Brookings Institution.

Carasso, Adam, C. Eugene Steuerle, and Elizabeth Bell. 2005. The trend in federal housing tax expenditures. *Tax Notes*. Washington, DC: Tax Policy Center of the Urban Institute and Brookings Institution.

Cheung, Steven N. S. 1974. A theory of price control. *Journal of Law and Economics* 17, no. 1: 53–71.

Citizens' Housing and Planning Association. 2006. Fact sheet on Chapter 40B. http://www.chapa.org/40b_fact.html.

Coleman, J. S., E. Q. Campbell, C. J. Hobson, F. McPartland, A. M. Mood, F. D. Weinfeld, et. al. 1966. *Equality of Educational Opportunity*. Washington, D.C.: U.S. Government Printing Office.

Congressional Budget Office. 2001. *Federal subsidies and the housing GSEs.* Washington, DC: Congress of the United States.

Cummings, Jean and Denise DiPasquale. 1999. The Low Income Housing Tax Credit: An analysis of the first ten years. *Housing Policy Debate* 10, no. 2: 251–307.

Cutler, David and Grant Miller. 2006. Water, water everywhere: Municipal finance and water supply in American cities. In *Corruption and reform: Lessons from America's economic history*, ed. Edward Glaeser and C. Goldin, 153–86. Chicago: University of Chicago Press.

Danter Company. 2006. Detailed allocations with estimated populations. http://www.danter.com/taxcredit/allocpop.htm.

———. 2008. Statistical overview of the LIHTC program, 1987–2005. http://www.danter.com/TAXCREDIT/stats.htm.

DiPasquale, D., and Edward Glaeser. 1999. Incentives and social capital: Are homeowners better citizens? *Journal of Urban Economics* 45, no. 2: 354–84.

Eriksen, Michael. 2007. Neighborhoods, risk, and the value of low income housing tax credits. Manuscript. Economics Department, Syracuse University.

Eriksen, Michael and Stuart Rosenthal. 2007. Crowd out, stigma, and the effect of place-based subsidized rental housing. Manuscript. Economics Department, Syracuse University.

Federal Reserve Board. 2006. Federal Reserve Statistical Release. Flow of Funds Accounts of the United States. Table B.100, Balance sheet of households and nonprofit organizations. www.federalreserve.gov/releases/z1/Current/z1r-5.pdf.

Fogelson, Robert M. 2007. *Bourgeois nightmares: Suburbia, 1870–1930.* New Haven, CT: Yale University Press.

Frankena, Mark. 1975. Alternative models of rent control. *Urban Studies* 12, no. 3: 303–8.

Frieden, Bernard. 1968. Housing and national urban goals: Old policies and new realities. In *The metropolitan enigma: Inquiries into the nature and dimensions of America's urban crisis,* ed. James Q. Wilson, 159–204. Cambridge, MA: Harvard University Press.

Friedman, Milton. 1962. *Capitalism and freedom.* Chicago: University of Chicago Press.

Glaeser, Edward. 1998. Should transfer payments be indexed to local price levels? *Regional Science and Urban Economics* 28, no. 1: 1–20.

Glaeser, Edward and Joseph Gyourko. 2003. The impact of zoning on housing affordability. *Economic Policy Review* 9, no. 2: 21–39.

———. 2005. Urban decline and durable housing. *Journal of Political Economy* 113, no. 2: 345–75.

———. 2006. Housing dynamics. Working Paper No. 12787, National Bureau of Economic Research, Cambridge, MA.

Glaeser, Edward, Joseph Gyourko, and Albert Saiz. 2008. Housing supply and housing bubbles. *Journal of Urban Economics* 64, no. 2: 198–217.

Glaeser, Edward, Joseph Gyourko, and Raven Saks. 2005. Why have house prices gone up? *American Economic Review* 95, no. 2: 329–33.

Glaeser, Edward and Dwight M. Jaffee. 2006. What to do about Fannie and Freddie? *Economists' Voice* 3, no. 7. http://www.bepress.com/ev/vol3/iss7/art5.

Glaeser, Edward and Erzo F. P. Luttmer. 2003. The misallocation of housing under rent control. *The American Economic Review* 93, no. 4: 1027–46.

Glaeser, Edward, Jenny Schuetz, and Byrce Ward. 2006. *Regulation and the rise of housing prices in Greater Boston*. Cambridge, MA: Pioneer Institute for Public Policy Research and Rappaport Institute for Greater Boston.

Glaeser, Edward and Jesse Shapiro. 2003. The benefits of the home mortgage interest deduction. In *Tax policy and the economy* 17, ed. James M. Poterba, 37–82. Cambridge, MA: MIT Press.

Glaeser, Edward and Bryce A. Ward. 2006. The causes and consequences of land use regulation: Evidence from Greater Boston. Working Paper No. W12601, National Bureau of Economic Research. Cambridge, MA.

Goodman, John and John Ittner. 1992. The accuracy of home owners' estimates of house value. *Journal of Housing Economics* 2: 338–57.

Green, Richard and Michelle White. 1997. Measuring the benefits of homeowning: Effects on children. *Journal of Urban Economics* 41, no. 3: 441–61.

Gyourko, Joseph. Forthcoming. Urban housing markets. In *Making cities work*, ed. Robert Inman. Princeton, NJ: Princeton University Press.

Gyourko, Joseph and Peter Linneman. 1989. Equity and efficiency aspects of rent control: An empirical study of New York City. *Journal of Urban Economics* 26, no. 1: 54–74.

———. 1990. Rent controls and rental housing quality: A note on the effects of New York City's old controls. *Journal of Urban Economics* 27, no. 3: 398–409.

Gyourko, Joseph and Albert Saiz. 2006. Construction costs and the supply of housing structure. *Journal of Regional Science* 46, no. 4: 661–80.

Gyourko, Joseph E., Albert Saiz, and Anita A. Summers. 2008a. A new measure of the local regulatory environment for housing markets: Wharton Residential Land Use Regulatory Index. *Urban Studies* 45, no. 3: 693–729.

———. 2008b. Wharton Residential Land Use Regulation Index. http://real.wharton.upenn.edu/~gyourko/Wharton_residential_land_use_reg.html.

Gyourko, Joseph and Todd Sinai. 2003. The spatial distribution of housing-related ordinary income tax benefits. *Real Estate Economics* 31, no. 4: 527–75.

Hsieh, Chan-Tai and Enrico Moretti. 2003. Can free entry be inefficient? Fixed commissions and social waste in the real estate industry. *Journal of Political Economy* 111, no. 5: 1076–1122.

Hughes, Mark Alan and Peter Vandoren. 1990. Social policy through land reform: New Jersey's Mount Laurel controversy. *Political Science Quarterly* 105, no. 1: 97–111.

Ihlanfeldt, Keith and G. Burge. 2006a. The effects of impact fees on multifamily housing construction. *Journal of Regional Science* 46, no. 1: 420–35.

———. 2006b. Impact fees and single-family home construction. *Journal of Urban Economics* 60, no. 2: 284–306.

Jaffee, Dwight. 2003. The interest rate risk of Fannie Mae and Freddie Mac. *Journal of Financial Services Research* 24, no. 1: 5–29.

Jencks, Christopher. 1994. *The homeless.* Cambridge, MA: Harvard University Press.

Katz, Lawrence, Jeffrey Kling, and Jeffrey Liebman. 2007. Experimental analysis of neighborhood effects. *Econometrica* 75, no. 1: 83–119.

Katz, Lawrence and Kenneth Rosen. 1987. The interjurisdictional effects of growth controls on housing prices. *Journal of Law and Economics* 30 (April): 149–60.

Kennedy, S. D. and M. Finkel. 1994. *Section 8 rental voucher and rental utilization study.* Washington, DC: U.S. Department of Housing and Urban Development. Office of Policy Development and Research.

Kirp, David, John Dwyer, and Larry Rosenthal. 1995. *Our town: Race, housing and the soul of suburbia.* New Brunswick, NJ: Rutgers University Press.

Krefetz, Sharon. n.d. The impact of Chapter 40B: The 1969 Massachusetts Comprehensive Permit and Zoning Appeals Act. Clark University, Worcester, MA. http://www.clarku.edu/activelearning/departments/government/krefetz/krefetz.cfm.

Laibson, David. 1997. Golden eggs and hyperbolic discounting. *Quarterly Journal of Economics* 112, no. 2: 443–77.

LexisNexis Municipal Codes. 2008. Marin County, CA County Code. http//municipalcodes.lexisnexis.com/codes/marincounty.

Lindbeck, Assar. 1977. *The political economy of the new Left.* New York: Harper and Row. (Orig. pub. 1971).

Listokin, David and David B. Hattis. 2005. Building codes and housing. *Cityscape: A Journal of Policy Development and Research* 8, no. 1: 21–67.

Lowry, S. 1983. *Experimenting with housing allowances: The final report of the Housing Assistance Supply Experiment.* Cambridge, MA: Oelgeschlager, Gunn, and Hain.

Maisel, S. J. 1953. *Housebuilding in transition: Based on studies in the San Francisco Bay Area.* Berkeley: University of California Press.

McKenzie, Joseph. 2002. A reconsideration of the jumbo/non-jumbo mortgage rate differential. *Journal of Real Estate Finance and Economics* 25, no. 2/3: 197–213.

Millennial Housing Commission. 2002. *Meeting our nation's housing challenges.* Washington, DC: GPO.

Muth, Richard F. and Elliot Wetzler. 1976. The effect of constraints on house costs. *Journal of Urban Economics* 3, no. 1: 57–67.

National Agency for Enterprise and Housing. 2004. *Housing statistics in the European Union 2003.* Copenhagen: European Union. July.

Noam, Eli M. 1983. The interaction of building codes and housing prices. *Journal of American Real Estate and Urban Economics Association* 10, no. 4: 394–403.

Nothaft, Frank, James Pearce, and Stevan Stevanovic. 2002. Debt spreads between GSEs and other corporations. *Journal of Real Estate Finance and Economics* 25, no. 2/3: 151–72.

Novak, William J. 1996. *The people's welfare: Law and regulation in nineteenth-century America.* Chapel Hill: University of North Carolina Press.

Office of Federal Housing Enterprise Oversight. 2006a. Table 2 Originations of conventional single family mortgages, 1990–2006 Q2. www.ofheo.gov/media/pdf/SFMortOutstanding1990to2006Q2.xls.

———. 2006b. Table 4 Single family mortgages outstanding, 1990–2006 Q2. www.ofheo.gov/media/pdf/SFMortOutstanding1990to2006Q2.xls.

O'Flaherty, Brendan. 1996. *Making room: The economics of homelessness.* Cambridge, MA: Harvard University Press.

Olsen, Edgar. 1972. An econometric analysis of rent control. *Journal of Political Economy* 80, no. 6: 1081–1100.

———. 2003. Housing programs for low income households. In *Means-tested transfer programs in the United States,* ed. Robert Moffitt, 365–442. Chicago: University of Chicago Press.

Passmore, Wayne, Roger Sparks, and Jamie Ingpen. 2002. GSEs, mortgage rates, and the long-run effects of mortgage securitization. *Journal of Real Estate Finance and Economics* 25, no. 2/3: 215–42.

Pollakowski, H. 1999. Rent regulation and housing maintenance in New York City. Working Paper #79, MIT Center for Real Estate, Cambridge, MA.

Poterba, James. 1992. Taxation and housing: Old questions, new answers. *American Economic Review* 82, no. 2: 237–42.

Poterba, James and Todd Sinai. 2008. Tax expenditures for owner-occupied housing: Deductions for property taxes and mortgage interest and the exclusion of imputed rental income. *American Economic Review,* forthcoming.

R. S. Means. 2008. *Assemblies Cost Data.* Kingston, MA: R. S. Means Company.

Roback, Jennifer. 1982. Wages, rents, and the quality of life. *Journal of Political Economy* 90, no. 6: 1257–78.

Rosen, Harvey. 1979. Housing decisions and the U.S. income tax. *Journal of Public Economics* 36, no. 1: 87–109.

Rosen, Sherwin. 1979. Wage-based indexes of urban quality of life. In *Current issues in urban economics,* ed. Peter Mieszkowski and Mahlon Straszheim, 74–104. Baltimore: Johns Hopkins University Press.

Saks, Raven. 2008. Job creation and housing construction: Constraints on metropolitan area employment growth. *Journal of Urban Economics* 64, no. 1: 178–195.

Seidel, Stephen R. 1978. *Housing costs & government regulations: Confronting the regulatory maze.* New Brunswick, NJ: Rutgers University, Center for Urban Policy Research.

Sinai, Todd and Joseph Gyourko. 2004. The (un)changing geographical distribution of housing tax benefits, 1980–2002. In *Tax policy and the economy* 18, ed. James M. Poterba, 175–208. Cambridge, MA: MIT Press.

Sinai, Todd and Joel Waldfogel. 2005. Do low-income housing subsidies increase the occupied stock? *Journal of Public Economics* 89, no. 11/12: 2137–64.

Susin, Scott. 2002. Rent voucher and the price of low-income housing. *Journal of Public Economics* 83, no. 1: 109–152.

U.S. Census Bureau. 2006a American FactFinder. Selected social characteristics in the United States, 2006. http://factfinder.census.gov/servlet/ADPTable?_bm=y&-geo_id=01000US&-qr_name=ACS_2006_EST_G00_DP2&-ds_name=ACS_2006_EST_G00_&-_lang=en&-_sse=on.

———. 2006b. American housing survey for the United States 2005. Washington, DC: GPO.

———. 2008. Characteristics of new housing. http://www.census.gov/const/www/charindex.html.

U.S. Congress. House of Representatives. Committee on Ways and Means. 2004. *2004 Green Book*, 108th Congress.

U.S. Department of Housing and Urban Development. 2007. Schedule B – FY 2007 final fair market rents for existing housing. http://www.huduser.org/datasets/fmr/fmrs/index.asp?data=fmr07.

U.S. General Accounting Office. 2002. *Federal housing assistance: Comparing the characteristics and costs of housing programs*. GAO-02-76. Washington, DC.

Von Hoffman, Alexander. 1998. The origins of American housing reform. Working paper, John F. Kennedy School of Government, Joint Center for Housing Studies, Taubman Center for State and Local Government, Harvard University, Cambridge, MA.

Wallace, James. 1995. Financing affordable housing in the United States. *Housing Policy Debate* 6, no. 4: 785–814.

About the Authors

Edward L. Glaeser is the Fred and Eleanor Glimp Professor of Economics at Harvard University, where he also serves as director of the Taubman Center for State and Local Government and director of the Rappaport Institute for Greater Boston. He has taught at Harvard since 1992, when he received his PhD from the University of Chicago. Professor Glaeser's research focuses on cities and housing, but he has also published papers on political economy, law and economics, and health-related behaviors. His most recent book is *Cities, Agglomeration and Spatial Equilibrium*, which was based on his Lindahl Lectures and published by Oxford University Press.

Joseph Gyourko is the Martin Bucksbaum Professor of Real Estate and Finance at the Wharton School of the University of Pennsylvania. He also serves as director of the Zell/Lurie Real Estate Center at Wharton and is chair of the Real Estate Department. Professor Gyourko received his BA from Duke University and a PhD in economics from the University of Chicago. His research interests include real estate finance, urban economics, and housing markets. Formerly coeditor of the journal *Real Estate Economics*, Professor Gyourko presently serves on a number of journal advisory and editorial boards. Finally, he is a trustee of the Urban Land Institute and is a member of the World Economic Forum's Global Agenda Council on the Future of Real Estate.

Index